ANNE DESJARDINS
COOKS AT L'EAU À LA BOUCHE

✻ THE SEASONAL CUISINE ✻
OF QUEBEC

L'EAU A LA BOUCHE

RELAIS &
CHATEAUX

ANNE DESJARDINS
COOKS <u>AT</u> L'EAU À LA BOUCHE

✻ THE SEASONAL CUISINE ✻
OF QUEBEC

Douglas & McIntyre

Vancouver / Toronto

03 04 05 06 07   5 4 3 2 1

Douglas & McIntyre
2323 Quebec Street, Suite 201
Vancouver, British Columbia
Canada V5T 4S7
www.douglas-mcintyre.com

National Library of Canada Cataloguing in Publication Data

Desjardins, Anne, 1951-
   Anne Desjardins cooks at L'eau à la bouche : the seasonal cuisine of
   Quebec / Anne Desjardins.

   Published also in French under title: L'eau à la bouche: les 4 saisons
   selon Anne Desjardins.
   ISBN 1-55365-020-4

1. Cookery—Quebec (Province)—Sainte-Adèle. 2. Eau à la bouche
(Restaurant)   I. Title.

TX945.5.E18D47 2003   641.5'09714'24   C2003-910573-3

Originated by Editions du Trécarré and published simultaneously in French under the title: *L'eau à la Bouche: Les 4 saisons selon Anne Desjardins*

Jacket and interior design by Cyclone Design Communications
Jacket and interior photography by Tango Photographie
Printed in China
Printed on acid-free paper

The publisher gratefully acknowledges the financial support of the Canada Council for the Arts, the British Columbia Arts Council, and the Government of Canada through the Book Publishing Industry Development Program (BPIDP) for its publishing activities.

ADDITIONAL CREDITS:
Photos of tomatoes and cows on page 111: Martin Auger (MAPAQ)
Photo on pages 154-155: Mary Hill Harpur
Photo of the restaurant entrance on page 111: Guillaume Poulliot
Photo on page 11: Guillaume Poulliot
Illustrations on end papers and pages 22-23: acrylics by Anne Desjardins

OTHER COOKS PRESENT DURING THE PHOTO SHOOT:
Luc Gilbert, Philippe Béliard, Guillaume Daigneault, Isabelle Yeung, Nancy Hinton,
Emmanuel Desjardins Richard.

Table of Contents

Anne Desjardins
and L'Eau à la Bouche

A LITTLE HISTORY

The opening of L'Eau à la Bouche in Ste.-Adèle at the end of the 1970s was a labour of love, one that combined a great deal of naïveté and idealism with an abiding passion for the pleasures of good food.

In December 1979, my partner, Pierre Audette, and I had just graduated in geography from the University of Quebec in Montreal when we found a lovely little house in Ste.-Adèle that had belonged to a German cabinetmaker with an eye for beauty. We decided to open a small bistro-style restaurant where we would serve simple but unusual dishes.

Why did we choose the Laurentians? It was a natural choice: it's a beautiful region that is not too far from Montreal, and it has attracted nature lovers and outdoor enthusiasts since the 1920s. When I was a child, it was where my family would spend summer vacations and weekends. My father's family comes from the region, and my great-grandfather Ferdinand Desjardins was one of the founders of the village of Canton-Marchand (the present-day L'Annonciation) in the late nineteenth century. A colonist with a penchant for adventure, he was lured to the Laurentians by Curé Labelle's promises of a better future.

And so we embarked on our adventure. We lived upstairs from the restaurant, which was practical since we had a five-year-old son, Emmanuel, and could look after him as we worked. I presided over the kitchen, inexperienced but full of good intentions, while Pierre served the customers. He quickly sensed their keen interest in sophisticated food and service, so we decided to hone our skills and expand our knowledge.

Luckily, one of the things we retained from going to school was learning how to learn. As I was a self-taught chef, I sought to learn all I could by taking numerous courses, subscribing to just about all the culinary publications of the time and starting a collection of cookbooks and reference works on cooking techniques, the science of cooking and the history of food. And I had ample opportunity to apply everything I learned.

The most important thing I discovered through the courses and workshops I took in France in the early 1980s was how passionate French chefs are about product quality and how obsessed they are with freshness. I was impressed by the diversity and regional character of the products they use, by their continual quest for excellence, by their pride in local products and by their sense of solidarity with growers and producers. This knowledge gave me the confidence I lacked and convinced me I was on the right track. Intuitively, I had always sought to create these same bonds with my suppliers, so that I too could offer only the very best products to my customers.

The years passed and we had another son, Félix. We dreamt of opening an inn, and it became a reality in June 1987. With my

The opening of L'Eau à la Bouche in Ste.-Adèle in the early 1980s was a labour of love, one that combined a great deal of naïveté and idealism with an abiding passion for the pleasures of good food.

**ANNE DESJARDINS
COOKS AT
L'EAU À LA BOUCHE**
THE SEASONAL CUISINE
OF QUEBEC

PAGE 9

father's help, we built a small, twenty-five-room hotel with tasteful decor next to the restaurant. Our little beds of herbs and edible flowers expanded to fill the additional property. In 1989, thanks to an energetic team effort by all the departments of our young company, we were asked to join the prestigious Relais & Châteaux network. It was an incredible honour.

I must say that cooking is one of the best jobs in the world. To prepare and share fine food, to surprise and delight my customers, is sheer magic.

Since Pierre and the dining room staff had developed an avid interest in wine, we expanded our wine cellar. Service at the hotel was warm, attentive and personalized. A great spirit of cooperation developed between the kitchen staff and the sommeliers, who worked together to create "discovery menus," matching our dishes with just the right wines.

From there, things moved along swiftly. Of course, family life continued throughout this eventful decade, with Pierre often taking care of Emmanuel and Félix. Our team expanded, as we hired skilled professionals who shared our philosophy.

In the 1990s, I was often invited to represent the cuisine of Quebec at gastronomy and tourism events in cities such as Toronto, Washington, New York, Paris, Barcelona, Cairo and Tokyo. I frequently took part in charity gourmet events and appeared on television and radio, and worked to develop a high-quality regional cuisine by teaching classes, taking on apprentices and collaborating with other chefs.

In 2001, L'Eau à la Bouche was designated a Relais Gourmand. I am particularly pleased to have received this honour, since the Relais Gourmands in the Relais & Châteaux network are recognized as leaders in the world of fine food, with chefs who work together with small-scale producers and growers. Most Relais Gourmands restaurants are owned by the chefs themselves and the chefs are often the second generation to devote themselves to fine cui-

sine. It is exactly this spirit that prevails at L'Eau à la Bouche. That same year, I was also honoured with the Renaud-Cyr award from the Quebec Ministry of Agriculture, which recognizes chefs who build close working relationships with their producers.

In 2002, I received the prestigious title of Chevalier de l'Ordre national du Québec. It was a first in the field of hostelry and cuisine, presented in recognition of my professional contribution to Quebec culture and its international profile.

Emmanuel, my older son (who literally grew up amid pots and pans), decided to study cooking at the École hôtelière des Laurentides and then gained experience through apprenticeships with other chefs of high repute. I was delighted when he joined the team at L'Eau à la Bouche. It's a thrill to work with a well-trained second-generation cook at my side.

I must say that cooking is one of the best jobs in the world. To prepare and share fine food, to surprise and delight my customers, is sheer magic.

A FEAST OF MEMORIES

It's a daunting task to try and summarize a quarter-century in the life of a chef in just a few pages. There's so much to say about the people who have accompanied me on this journey.

Good chefs are made, not born, to paraphrase an old adage. Chance, family and upbringing all have a hand in determining the courses our lives will follow. We started out with a modest little country restaurant and great faith in the future, and we embarked on an adventure in which we could have easily succumbed to the many pitfalls that await intrepid neophytes in the restaurant business.

As a child, I never gave any thought to becoming a cook, yet even at an early age, I loved good food. Many of my most vivid

**ANNE DESJARDINS
COOKS AT
L'EAU À LA BOUCHE**
THE SEASONAL CUISINE
OF QUEBEC

PAGE 11

childhood memories revolve around family meals and the pleasures of the table.

My grandmother Raymonde was a talented and intuitive cook. She was also an outstanding hostess. Everyone who dined at her table can attest to her generosity and sophistication, not to mention her mouthwatering dishes. She had a knack for choosing only the best and the freshest products. She shopped at small pastry shops, butcher shops and local farms where, every season, she would buy natural honey, maple syrup, vegetables and berries to make jam.

My father loved to travel. My two sisters and I looked forward to family trips with great delight. We visited the breathtakingly beautiful Gaspé Peninsula and North Shore of Quebec. We feasted on lobster, shrimps, clams and freshly caught fish in the Maritimes and on the east coast of the United States. We fell under the intense spell of New York City. We explored Europe, with its rich history, magnificent landscapes and myriad cultures living side by side. Even back then, I was curious and eager to try new dishes and experience new tastes and smells. I vividly remember my first perfectly ripe fresh fig and fritto misto in Italy, and the crisp, succulent calamari I first tried in Greece.

In my early twenties, I experimented with recipes and enjoyed trying them out on my friends. While I was in university, I took great pleasure in roaming along Montreal's St. Laurent Boulevard in search of rare or obscure ingredients and fresh produce. I spent hours in natural food stores, where I discovered various types of organic flours and little-known beans and legumes. Sometimes, I would venture further afield, exploring small oriental grocery stores in Chinatown, redolent with ginger and star anise and chock-full of exotic vegetables. I think I spent almost as much time inventing and testing recipes as I did studying geography!

Once my husband and I had graduated, our dream of opening a restaurant in the country began to take shape. Although he

had his doubts about the project, my father agreed to support us. With his financial help and sage counsel, we were able to open a small restaurant on the highway that runs through Ste.-Adèle, a scenic little resort village north of Montreal. It was here that we put our ideas to the test. At first, both of our families were a bit alarmed by our choice. The restaurant business is hardly what you would call relaxing and, on top of it all, we had absolutely no experience.

We enrolled at the Institut de tourisme et d'hôtellerie du Québec in Montreal (ITHQ) for a few well-designed seminars on hotel management and transformed the house we had bought into a restaurant. We got all the necessary permits, did the construction work, developed the menu and bought professional kitchen and dining room equipment. We even made our own lampshades out of rice paper! Now all we needed was a name for the restaurant. It was Pierre who came up with *L'Eau à la Bouche* (mouthwatering). With the enthusiastic support, astute advice and steadfast support of my father-in-law, André Audette, and encouragement from our family and friends, we were finally ready to open our doors.

From the very beginning, we attracted customers with an interest in fresh food and original dishes. The late 1970s and early 1980s were something of a turning point. Back then, it was almost unheard of to serve broccoli or sugar-snap peas al dente. Equally novel were fiddleheads and wild garlic, toasted sesame seeds, chicken breasts in a herb sauce that had not been thickened with flour and serving a cheese plate at the end of the meal. We used the freshest ingredients we could find and prepared everything on the premises, with no commercial additives or products.

To get an idea of how far we have come in Quebec, consider that, in 1980, just trying to find fresh, locally grown products was an adventure in itself. The suppliers back then found us very demanding and couldn't understand what we were looking for: "What do you mean? Our products aren't good enough for you?" Countless times I was told that such-and-such a famous chef found a particular product—which I felt was mediocre—to be excellent. Restaurant food in the late 1970s was most often inspired by the great classics of French cooking (usually prepared with a heavy hand, using products of ordinary quality) or else it was "Continental" cuisine, with huge slabs of steak, previously frozen garlic-broiled langoustines, baked potatoes and Provençal tomatoes masquerading as gourmet fare.

In the early days, I was lucky to have many well-informed and well-travelled customers who appreciated fine food and encouraged me in my efforts. Some of them became my most loyal supporters, inviting their gourmet clubs to the restaurant or sponsoring some of my professional development seminars in France. Although I cannot name them all here, I am especially grateful to Mr. and Mrs. Bernard Lamarre, Maurice Dufresne and Jean-Guy Blanchette.

As luck would have it, Ste.-Adèle became the site of the new École hôtelière des Laurentides in the early 1980s. The school's director, Phillipe Belleteste, was an open-minded and accommodating man with a highly professional vision of the métier. There were a few of us in the Laurentians who were eager to hone our professional skills. I have fond memories of the friendships I developed with Louise Duhamel, Jean-Louis Massenavette, Léopold Handfield and others.

Paule Neyrat of the Fondation Auguste Escoffier in Villeneuve Loubet, France, gave me permission to take part in the prestigious Chefs pour Chefs seminars. I'll never forget the experience of watching André Daguin, Jacques Chibois, Michel Lorain, Émile Jung and Gérard Vié as they shared their knowledge and their vision of cooking.

The Institut de tourisme et d'hôtellerie du Québec, headed by Antoine Samueli, is a dynamic institution. Energetic, forward-looking instructors like Jean-Paul Grappe and Jean-Claude Belmont have made it a leader in its field.

Among my memorable experiences in the 1980s were the introductory courses in sommellerie, or wine stewardship, that my husband and I took with Jacques Orhon at the École hôtelière des Laurentides. These courses led me to make some amazing discoveries, and I developed a whole new approach to taste. I changed the way I composed my sauces, giving them new depth and structure. We also began to pay close attention to matching our dishes with the right wines.

Looking back, I realize that the 1980s went by quickly. New information and new trends sprung up everywhere. Committees, clubs and associations were formed, journalists helped popularize the new culinary diversity and reticence gradually gave way to a more open-minded attitude.

In about 1986, the Quebec Ministry of Agriculture got involved. Rose-Hélène

To get an idea of how far we have come in Quebec, consider that, in 1980, just trying to find fresh, locally grown products was an adventure in itself.

ANNE DESJARDINS
COOKS AT
L'EAU À LA BOUCHE
THE SEASONAL CUISINE
OF QUEBEC

PAGE 13

Coulombe put an incredible amount of energy into fostering the emergence of a "new" regional Quebec cuisine. It took considerable effort to initiate something that we take for granted today. I have no desire to recount the long, convoluted history of the Corporation de la cuisine régionale du Québec, but I would like to acknowledge the invaluable contribution made by the members of this association. Food writers like Françoise Keller and Julian Armstrong were witnesses of that evolution. The present-day "Tables de concertation agroalimentaire" evolved directly out of these initiatives. The creation of these consultation committees is due in large part to the ability of people like Martin Auger from the Quebec Ministry of Agriculture to rally support, and also to the energy and tenacity of Jean Audette, commissioner of the Table de concertation des Laurentides. His close ties with the region's producers and growers have encouraged vital cooperation between chefs and suppliers.

I often compare my profession to acting. Whether you're in the kitchen or on stage, you need to know your lines, your recipes…

I am a firm believer in continuing education. I think people love to learn and discover. The stimulating nature of learning and knowledge is a powerful force in the quest for pleasure and the desire to excel. In this profession, as in most others, we find pleasure in working very hard at what we do. Above all, we must not be afraid to continually question what we know.

Of course, cooking also involves a little magic. I have been fortunate enough to meet many cooks, both professionals and amateurs. I recognize that some of us have an empirical approach, an instinct, a flair that seems to have more to do with magic than with technical know-how. And yet the results are good—excellent even.

I often compare my profession to acting. Whether you're in the kitchen or on stage, you need to know your lines (recipes); you need a good memory and unshakeable concentration. You need good technique but you also need unlimited reserves of energy, because when the curtain rises (the restaurant door opens) and the show (the meal) begins, you have to be ready. Whatever happens, "the show must go on." It's thrilling and magical. I get a huge adrenaline rush as the first customers arrive. We know we have a great product, and every dish we serve is meticulously prepared. We have skilled and experienced employees who are passionate about what they do. We're ready to welcome our guests and treat them to a sublime experience that will leave them with delicious memories.

We have to challenge our ideas about taste and seek out the freshest possible products—in season, of course. We have to be in tune with our times. We have to cook with the aim of giving pleasure and sharing the finer things in life. The guests who choose to eat at our restaurant are doing us an honour, and we must bear that in mind at all times. For all of these reasons, I maintain a close relationship with our producers and growers.

I believe our gamble has paid off. Most local chefs now accept the idea that regional products have much to offer. In return, producers have understood the advantages of having their products featured by chefs.

In the late 1980s, Antoine Samueli and René Fortin of the Ministry of Tourism had the ingenious idea of inviting Quebec chefs to take part in promotional campaigns outside Canada to showcase their savoir-faire. This was another giant step forward, since it enabled us to show off the vitality, originality and distinctive character of our approach to cooking. Quebec cuisine finally shook off its heavy, old-fashioned image, which had been shaped by ancient traditions and our rural subsistence economy.

The cuisine we know and love today grew out of a small, rather elitist trend that emerged in France in the early 1970s. Its originators were restaurant owners who were also chefs (Troisgros, Bocuse, Barrier, Pic). Since they owned their own restau-

SOME HIGHLIGHTS ALONG THE WAY

1987: Winner of the Dîner de l'Année, awarded by the International Wine and Food Society in Canada

Since 1989: Certified member of Relais & Châteaux

Since 1990: Recognized with the Distinguished Restaurants of North America (DiRoNA) award of excellence

1995: Anne cooks for the James Beard Foundation in New York

1995: L'Eau à la Bouche is the subject of a *New York Times Magazine* cover story by Molly O'Neill

1995 to 1998: Recipient of the Prestige de la Table au Québec, awarded by the Société des Alcools du Québec (Quebec's liquor control board)

1996 to 1999: *Gourmet* magazine names L'Eau à la Bouche as one of the top five restaurants in the Montreal area, in "America's Top Tables" (awarded first place in 1996, 1997 and 1998)

1998: Winner of the Table d'Or, awarded by Tourisme-Québec

Since 1998: Recipient of the Award of Excellence presented by *Wine Spectator*

1999 to 2000: Member of the Canadian Airlines Chefs' Conclave

Since 2000: Winner of the Mobil four-star award

Since 2001: L'Eau à la Bouche is named a Relais Gourmand, in addition to being a member of Relais & Châteaux

2002: Anne receives the Renaud-Cyr award and is named Chevalier de l'Ordre national du Québec

rants, they were free to experiment and to develop their recipes and menus.

This trend was in keeping with the spirit of the times, which was marked by changing attitudes toward health and travel, coupled with less restrictive trade relations. Chefs began to take classic recipes and simplify them (Michel Guérard with his cuisine minceur, for example). They served dishes in more sophisticated presentations and experimented with new ingredients that were often Asian or tropical in origin. This came to be known as Nouvelle Cuisine, a term often used pejoratively and even more often

badly interpreted by inept cooks. Over time, it evolved into "eclectic cuisine" and "market cuisine" and, in the hands of creative North American chefs, has become known as "fusion cuisine" (sometimes more aptly called "confusion").

The winds of change have swept through the culinary world. I believe Quebec has played a leading role in North America. In terms of this open-minded approach to cooking and the rediscovery of little-known but delectable regional products, we *are* the cutting edge.

Fromagerie Le p'tit train du Nord

SEASONAL CUISINE AT L'EAU À LA BOUCHE

At L'Eau à la Bouche, we are committed to cooking with the seasons. The dramatic seasonal changes of our northern climate offer numerous possibilities to the inventive chef: diversity, quality and inspiration. A problem can be turned into an advantage, thanks to technological advances and the know-how of northern growers and producers.

I describe my cooking as regional, because it is defined by a place. Put simply, I can say that I cook in Ste.-Adèle, in the Laurentians, in Quebec, in Canada, in North America, at the forty-seventh parallel.

I enjoy cooking with fresh products and like to know where they come from. Over the years, I have realized that I get more pleasure from using products that have a story behind them, especially when I get to know the people who grow or produce them. Not only that, I cook better and am more inspired if I can get a feel for the produce.

This quest for fresh local products and my northern location have inspired my cooking and given it its distinctive character. For more than twenty years, the high quality of Quebec-grown products and my close relationships with small-scale producers have encouraged me to harmonize my cooking with the seasons. I take great pride in talking about Quebec products—particularly those from the Laurentians—and in featuring them in my recipes.

Each season brings distinctive offerings, and we often have an abundance of riches to choose from. Recent years have seen the emergence of a new generation of producers who are more open-minded than the last and increasingly aware of Canadians' changing eating habits. This shift has resulted in a profusion of delicious, well-made products that chefs are keen to use. We have only to pick and choose our ingredients and create innovative, mouth-watering dishes.

**ANNE DESJARDINS
COOKS AT
L'EAU À LA BOUCHE**
THE SEASONAL CUISINE
OF QUEBEC

PAGE 17

Basics

I like to add most spices and herbs—such as pepper, thyme and rosemary—to stocks and sauces to ensure a fresh taste and acccording to the needs of each dish. Therefore, I have generally omitted them from the basic recipes.

FLAVOURFUL POULTRY STOCK

MAKES 1 LITRE (4 CUPS)

Ingredients

1 kg	poultry bones (chicken, duck, quail, pigeon, turkey, goose, guinea fowl)	2 lb
	vegetable oil	
500 mL	mirepoix (finely diced carrots, celery, leeks *or* onions)	2 cups
50 mL	white wine vinegar	3 tbsp
500 mL	white wine	2 cups
5	parsley sprigs	5
	celery leaves	
2	bay leaves	2

Preparation

1. Using a cleaver, cut up the bones. Brown in a little vegetable oil in a stockpot over high heat. Add the mirepoix and caramelize. Deglaze with the vinegar and wine.

2. Fill the stockpot with enough water to cover the bones. Add the parsley sprigs, celery leaves and bay leaves, and simmer for an hour or so, until reduced by half. Do not stir the stock. Strain, let cool and refrigerate.

3. This stock will keep for 4 to 5 days in the refrigerator. It can also be frozen.

FLAVOURFUL VEAL STOCK

MAKES 2 LITRES (8 CUPS)

Ingredients

3 kg	veal bones (shanks, marrow bones, etc.)	6 ½ lb
	vegetable oil	
500 mL	mirepoix (finely diced carrots and leeks *or* onions and celery)	2 cups
50 mL	good-quality red wine vinegar	3 tbsp
500 mL	red wine	2 cups
	parsley sprigs	
	celery leaves	

Preparation

1. Place the bones in a roasting pan and brown in a very hot oven (200°C [400°F]), with a little vegetable oil. Add the mirepoix and continue browning. Deglaze with the vinegar and wine.

2. Place all the ingredients in a large stockpot, over medium heat. Add enough water to cover the bones. Add the parsley sprigs and the celery stalks and leaves. Simmer until reduced by half. Do not stir the stock. Strain, let cool and refrigerate.

3. This stock will keep for 4 to 5 days in the refrigerator. It can also be frozen.

FLAVOURFUL FISH AND SHELLFISH STOCK

MAKES 1 LITRE (4 CUPS)

Ingredients

1 kg	shrimp, crab and lobster shells	2 lb
	or	
1 kg	bones and heads of white-fleshed fish	2 lb
	or	
1 kg	live mussel and clam shells	2 lb
	vegetable oil	
2	stalks celery, finely diced	2
1	leek or onion, finely diced	1
1	red pepper (or equivalent in red pepper trimmings, for lobster, crab, shrimp stock), coarsely chopped	1
2	tomatoes, quartered	2
	juice of 1 lemon	
250 mL	white vermouth	1 cup
50 mL	pastis	3 tbsp
	parsley, celery and fennel leaves	

Preparation

1. Using a cleaver, crush the fish bones or shells. Brown in a little vegetable oil in a stockpot, over high heat. Add the vegetables and tomato. Deglaze with the lemon juice, vermouth and pastis.

2. Fill the stockpot with enough water to cover the shells. Add the parsley, celery and fennel leaves. Simmer until reduced by half. Do not stir the stock. Strain, let cool and refrigerate.

3. This stock will keep for 4 to 5 days in the refrigerator. It can also be frozen.

FRESH PASTA

This recipe calls for almost double the number of eggs suggested in traditional pasta recipes, but the difference they make to the taste is well worth it.

MAKES ENOUGH DOUGH FOR 36 SMALL RAVIOLI, 36 SMALL CANNELLONI OR SIX 60-G (2-OZ) SERVINGS OF TAGLIATELLE

Ingredients

230 g	best-quality bread flour (durum wheat flour)	½ lb
1	egg	1
6	egg yolks	6
15 mL	whole milk	1 tbsp
20 mL	extra-virgin olive oil	1 ½ tbsp

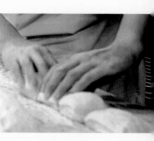

Preparation

1. Mound the flour on a work surface or in a big mixing bowl and make a well in the centre of the flour. Put the egg and egg yolks in the well and slowly mix them into the flour.

2. Add the milk and olive oil; knead well. When the dough loses its bright yellow colour, you'll know you have kneaded it sufficiently. It should be smooth and elastic but still moist.

3. Wrap the dough well in plastic wrap and refrigerate for at least 2 hours, and for up to a day.

GOAT'S MILK CHEDDAR TUILES

MAKES 6 TUILES

90g	grated goat's milk cheddar cheese (or substitute Parmesan Reggiano)	6 ½ oz

Preparation

Preheat the oven to 190°C (375°F). On a small baking sheet covered with parchment paper, mound grated cheese in circles 8 cm (3 in.) in diameter. Cook for about 5 minutes, or until golden brown. Cool and set aside.

ANNE DESJARDINS
COOKS AT
L'EAU À LA BOUCHE
THE SEASONAL CUISINE
OF QUEBEC

VEAL SWEETBREADS

Like liver and kidneys, sweetbreads are considered organ meat. The veal sweetbread is a growth gland that atrophies as the calf matures into a cow. Veal sweetbreads are highly coveted by connoisseurs, but many people are unfamiliar with them.

In our family, sweetbreads were served on festive occasions. Our favourite recipe was sweetbreads with mushrooms and cream, a delicious dish that melts in the mouth, and is full of delicately flavoured mushrooms and studded with tender pieces of sweetbread. I was so fond of it that it became the first sweetbread dish I served at the restaurant.

The main problems that amateur cooks encounter when preparing sweetbreads are finding high-quality, fresh lobes of heart sweetbreads (also called kernels) and cleaning (or deveining) them properly.

Here's a basic recipe for veal sweetbreads. You can adjust it to suit seasonal ingredients and your own inspiration, as we do at L'Eau à la Bouche. For example, we might use sherry vinegar and dry sherry instead of the wine, and add morels, or we might use a splash of Pernod in addition to the white wine, then add some star anise and serve the sweetbreads alongside Terry Hussey's baby carrots and fennel.

6 SERVINGS (AS AN APPETIZER)

Ingredients

1 kg	fresh veal heart sweetbreads	2 lb
	clarified butter	
	salt, to taste	
250 mL	mirepoix (finely diced celery and onions *or* leeks and carrots)	1 cup
25 mL	white wine vinegar	1 ⅔ tbsp
100 mL	white wine	⅜ cup
15 mL	chopped fresh garlic	1 tbsp
	parsley sprigs	
500 mL	veal stock (see page 18)	2 cups

Preparation

1. Choose the best sweetbreads you can find. They should be round and firm, without too many veins.

2. Soak in salted water for about 4 hours. Drain.

3. Preheat the oven to 160°C (325°F).

4. Clean the sweetbreads, using a small, sharp knife to remove all veins and fat.

5. Melt the clarified butter in a heavy-bottomed ovenproof skillet. Add the sweetbreads and sauté on each side over medium heat, until nicely browned. Season with salt. Remove from skillet and set aside.

6. Add the mirepoix to the skillet and brown lightly. Deglaze with the wine vinegar and add the white wine. Add the garlic, parsley, veal stock and sweetbreads.

7. Place in the oven and bake for about 20 minutes.

8. Remove from the oven. Take the sweetbreads out of the skillet and set aside. Strain the cooking juices into a small saucepan and simmer over medium heat until reduced by half. Allow to cool. The sweetbreads are now ready to be used in another recipe. Whole and well covered, they will keep 2 days in the refrigerator. To serve them alone as an appetizer, slice and pan-sear for a crispy finish, using the cooking liquor as a base for a sauce, or reheat in the cooking liquor and finish with cream and desired seasoning.

CREAMY OLIVE OIL EMULSION

This sauce, which I developed at L'Eau à la Bouche, is delicious and easy to make. The key is getting the proportions right.

Going against culinary tradition, I use two different fats here — olive oil and cream. I add an acid ingredient (which could be either a fine vinegar or the juice of a citrus fruit), salt and a few flavourings. The result is a sauce that will enhance the taste of many recipes. It's one that I make in diverse ways, depending on what ingredients inspire me the most.

I bring the sauce to a boil just before serving, so as not to spoil the taste of the olive oil.

6 SERVINGS

Ingredients

90 mL	good-quality extra-virgin olive oil	¼ cup
65 mL	35% cream	⅓ cup
30 mL	lemon *or* other citrus juice (*or* natural cider, *or* good-quality wine, *or* sherry)	2 tbsp
	salt, to taste	
	Tabasco sauce	

Preparation

1. Combine all ingredients.

2. Bring to a boil and heat for about half a minute (no more).

3. Add your own choice of ingredients to make your own version of this sauce.

SPICED MEAD CARAMEL

I developed this recipe when I discovered the wonderful mead, or honey wine, being produced in my region. I always keep some on hand. This mead and honey "caramel" is very useful for sweet and sour preparations. It's not overly sweet and will keep in the fridge for many weeks.

Ingredients

175 mL	Cuvée du Diable mead (or sweet, floral, oak-aged white wine)	⅝ cup
180 mL	wildflower honey	¾ cup
125 mL	white wine vinegar	½ cup

Spices

2 g	black peppercorns	1 tsp
2 g	allspice	1 tsp
2 g	pink peppercorns	1 tsp
2 g	whole cardamom	1 tsp
2 g	star anise	1 tsp
2 g	juniper berries	1 tsp

Preparation

1. Boil the mead for about 10 minutes in a small pot.

2. Using a mortar and pestle or a grinder, grind the spices and steep 4/5 of the resulting powder in the mead. Filter and set aside.

3. Cook the honey to the soft-ball stage (115°C [240°F]) for about 5 minutes. Remove from heat and stop the cooking process by adding the vinegar.

4. Boil for about 4 minutes, add the spiced mead and cook for another 4 minutes to thicken slightly. Remove from the heat and add the remaining spices. The consistency should be that of liquid caramel sauce when at room temperature.

Spring

By the end of March, the snow begins to melt and the days grow warmer and longer. But the nights are still chilly, and this makes the sap flow in the sugar maples. This phenomenon is a good example of how our northern climate brings gifts to the gourmet table. Not all varieties of maple go through this transformation; it really is our specific climate that awakens the sugar maple and brings forth its delectable liquid for just a few short weeks.

After the long cold months of snow and darkness, it is comforting to feel the weather warm up, to hear the nesting birds singing at dawn, to inhale the freshness of rushing streams and the woods as they come to life, and to feast our eyes on the budding trees, with their palette of tender greens, whites, pale pinks and bright yellows.

Well before the trees are in leaf, the woods abound with early delicacies. The first to find their way into my kitchen are the wild shoots gathered in the woods and fields and along riverbanks and lakeshores by François Brouillard, a skilled and meticulous collector whom I have nicknamed My Vagabond of the Woods. He forages for early fiddleheads, dogtooth violet leaves and cattail shoots.

From the Abitibi-Témiscaming region, I get northern morels. The earth exhales the odour of humus, the forests are covered in pale green down and we are all touched by nature's rebirth. The chives in my garden send up hundreds of vigorous green shoots that seem to double in height twice a day. The perennial violas are already thriving, creating splashes of brilliant colour here and there. I always look forward to using them to add little touches of yellow and purple to our salads.

In April, the fishing season gets underway in the Gulf of St. Lawrence, and this means superb, delicate snow crab and sweet little Nordic shrimps that melt in your mouth. Finally, in May, lobster arrives in our cold waters. I believe it is simply the best available, even though I know our French friends swear by Breton lobster. I may be biased, but I will dare to contradict them and state that the lobster caught off our shores is sweeter and more tender. It's so exciting to be able to use these treasures of the sea in recipes that bring out their flavour to best advantage.

The first crops harvested by the market gardeners in the Lower Laurentians are green and white asparagus. As soon as they become available, their fresh, slightly acid flavour is a welcome addition to our dishes.

And then there's rhubarb. How many people know that the Lower Laurentians is Quebec's largest rhubarb producing area? The variety known as Serbi, which Serge Bigras grows on his farm, is an incredible deep red. I love rhubarb for its inimitable, pleasantly sour taste. I use it in one recipe along with caramelized onions and Indonesian long pepper, which I serve with a pan-fried escalope of fresh duck foie gras, or with a venison terrine. Rhubarb, with its fruity taste and high acidity, enhances the richness of foie gras. It's also perfect for tempering overly sweet ingredients such as the ripe strawberries and Italian meringue in one of our current desserts.

Ste.-Anne-des-Plaines and St.-Joseph-du-Lac in the Lower Laurentians are hotbeds of berry production. By St. Jean Baptiste Day (June 24), we are feasting on succulent strawberries that burst with flavour. There are numerous varieties, and we now have strawberries right into fall with the growing use of ever-bearing plants. As summer settles in, there is a succession of berries and stone-fruit—raspberries, cherries, dewberries, serviceberries, Saskatoon berries, gooseberries, blackberries, black currants, wild blueberries—all of which find their way into our dishes. In both sweet and savoury recipes, we use berries like musical notes to accentuate the flavours.

DANIEL BAILLARD, IN HIS GREENHOUSE IN MIRABEL

Duo

Atlantic Lobster Medley with Cauliflower "Semolina," Coriander and Ginger

and

Scallop Tartare with Témiscaming Trout Caviar

I always enjoy serving my customers a duo or a composition of several elements that reflect different ways of handling the same culinary theme. In this case, I was inspired by freshwater and saltwater fish and seafood, but also by the spring season and its new lobster catch.

In another season, I might take a different approach to serving a duo, such as focusing on mushrooms rather than fish in the fall.

Atlantic Lobster Medley with Cauliflower "Semolina", Coriander and Ginger

This fairly easy-to-make recipe is delicious and looks spectacular. Serve it as the first course of an elegant meal or add more greens to create a summery main course. At the restaurant, we add fresh coriander shoots and cubes of jellied lobster stock and garnish the plates with lobster heads.

4 SERVINGS

Ingredients

90 mL	extra-virgin olive oil	6 tbsp
15 mL	grated fresh ginger	1 tbsp
1 bunch	fresh coriander	1 bunch
	salt, to taste	
1	large Atlantic lobster (675 g or 1 ½ lb)	1
	or	
250 g	cooked Atlantic lobster meat	½ lb
½	fresh cauliflower	½
	juice of 1 lemon	
½	red pepper	½
3	green onions	3
	Tabasco sauce	
80 g	orange flying fish roe, also called tobiko (optional)	3 oz

Preparation

1. Cook and shell the lobster. (The shells and innards can be saved to make a concentrated stock for another use.) Cut up the lobster meat, reserving the claws for garnish. Refrigerate.

2. Separate the cauliflower florets and, using a food processor, pulse to a fine, grainy texture that resembles a coarse semolina.

3. Place in a bowl and pour two-thirds of the lemon juice over the cauliflower semolina. Refrigerate.

Assembly

4. *Chop 10 mL (2 tsp) coriander and add to the remaining 10 mL (2 tsp) ginger. Finely dice the red pepper and thinly slice the green onion.*

5. *Fifteen minutes before serving, combine the lobster meat with 50 mL (3 tbsp) olive oil, the rest of the lemon juice and half the ingredients from step 7. Add a few drops of Tabasco. Set aside.*

6. *Combine the cauliflower semolina with 50 mL (3 tbsp) olive oil, the rest of the ingredients from step 7 and the flying fish roe (optional). Season with salt and Tabasco to taste. Set aside.*

7. *To serve, place the semolina on chilled plates (in round moulds, if possible). Top each serving with lobster meat, a half claw and a small coriander leaf.*

Duo of Fish and Seafood Appetizers

Scallop Tartare
with Témiscaming Trout Caviar

INGREDIENTS

1 bunch	fresh chives (about 20)	1 bunch
30 mL	best-quality virgin olive oil	2 tbsp
	salt, to taste	
15 mL	Dijon mustard	1 tbsp
½	cucumber, peeled and seeded	½
125 g	fresh scallops, well cleaned, muscle removed	4 ½ oz
	zest and juice of 1 lime	
	Tabasco sauce	
40 g	red trout caviar (or genuine black sturgeon caviar)	1 ½ oz

Preparation

1. Dice the cucumber and the scallops. Mince the chives. Refrigerate.

Assembly

2. Fifteen minutes before serving, combine the diced cucumber, scallops and chives with the olive oil and lime zest and juice. Add mustard, season with salt and a few drops of Tabasco. Correct the seasoning, if necessary.

3. Spoon the scallop mixture into 4 round moulds. Top with spoonfuls of emulsion and caviar. Place on chilled plates, remove the moulds.

Magdalen Islands Lobster
Poached in Beurre Monté with Sautéed Leeks, Green Asparagus, Morels and Coral Sauce

 This recipe is somewhat time-consuming to prepare but lobster lovers find it irresistible, and the vegetables give it a definite spring flavour. The trick is to leave yourself enough time for the first two steps. Coral is the name given to the unfertilized eggs of a female lobster, which become reddish when cooked.

4 SERVINGS

INGREDIENTS

2	lobsters, 750 g (1 ½ lb) each	2
450 g	unsalted butter, cubed	1 lb
	water	
	salt, to taste	
	Tabasco sauce	
	lemon juice	
20 (200 g)	large morels, cleaned	20 (7 oz)
½	leek, thinly sliced	½
12 stalks	asparagus, cut diagonally into 1.5-cm (½-in.) pieces	12 stalks

Preparation

1. Boil enough water to cover the two lobsters. Submerge them in the boiling water for 4 minutes, with the heat turned off. Remove from the water.

2. Detach the carapaces and tails, and submerge them in ice water. Return the claws to the boiling water for another 5 minutes and then submerge them in the ice water too. The shells will just be starting to turn red.

3. Drain and shell the lobster pieces, taking care to preserve the shape of the flesh, which will still be transparent since it is only partially cooked. Slice each of the 4 claws and 2 tails in half lengthwise. Refrigerate these pieces along with the innards (green) and any eggs (dark green).

4. Bring a 4-L (16-cup) pot of generously salted water to a boil. Add asparagus and cook until tender but still firm, about 2 to 3 minutes. Refresh in ice water. Pat dry.

5. To prepare the beurre monté, bring 450 mL (1 ¾ cups) water to a boil and add three-quarters of the butter cubes, whisking gently. Salt generously; add a few drops of Tabasco, a squeeze of lemon, and transfer to a double boiler to keep warm.

Assembly

6. Warm the plates in a low-temperature oven. When you are ready to serve, put the lobster meat in the beurre monté and poach gently for 5 minutes until the meat turns opaque. Using a double boiler prevents overcooking, because the temperature does not exceed 90°C (190°F). The protein can coagulate without the toughening that occurs when the temperature rises above 100°C (212°F).

7. In the meantime, melt a few of the remaining cubes of butter in another skillet and sauté the morels and leeks for a few minutes. Add the blanched asparagus and sauté briefly. Sprinkle the mixture with salt and arrange the vegetables on the heated plates.

8. To prepare the coral sauce, remove 150 mL (⅝ cup) of the beurre monté and put it into a separate bowl. Add 60 mL (¼ cup) of the lobsters' innards and eggs. Whisk gently, then taste and adjust the seasoning as necessary. Return to heat if necessary, whisking gently until the coral is cooked and the sauce turns red.

9. Place the lobster meat (half a tail and a claw) on top of the vegetables on each plate. Top with the sauce.

Magdalen Islands Lobster

Pan-seared Escalope
of Fresh Duck Foie Gras with Rhubarb and Onion Salsa, and Sweet and Sour Sauce

I've found a producer of fresh duck foie gras in Chambly, south of Montreal. Pascal and Francette Fleury of Ferme Palmex produce a very high-quality product. This foie gras is superbly flavourful, tricky to work with and costs a fortune. As recently as the early 1980s, no one was producing foie gras in Quebec. Now, I can serve foie gras at any time of the year.

4 SERVINGS

INGREDIENTS

1	shallot, minced	1
500 g	Serbi red rhubarb from the lower Laurentians (about 3 stalks), diced and macerated in 125 mL (½ cup) sugar for at least half a day	2 ½ cups
8	large long peppercorns (from Madagascar or Indonesia, or another variety), 4 of which are ground into a coarse powder	8
75 mL	natural cider vinegar	5 tbsp
200 mL	cider	¾ cup
400 mL	duck stock (or poultry stock, reduced) (see page 18)	1 ⅝ cups
1	onion, chopped	1
30 ml	olive oil	2 tbsp
4	raw fresh duck foie gras escalopes, 100 g (3 ½ oz) each	4

Preparation

1. *In a small saucepan, brown the shallot with 125 mL (½ cup) of the macerated rhubarb in olive oil over medium heat. Add a pinch of the ground long pepper.*

2. *Deglaze with the cider vinegar. Add the cider and reduce until almost dry. Add the stock and reduce again. When there is 300 mL (1 ¼ cups) of the liquid remaining, strain and season with salt to taste. Add the 4 long peppercorns and set aside.*

3. *In a skillet, sauté the onion in the remaining olive oil until golden. Add the remaining 500 mL (2 cups) rhubarb and the remaining crushed long pepper to complete the salsa. Do not overcook. Season with salt to taste. Keep warm.*

Assembly

4. *To serve, sear the escalopes of foie gras in a nonstick skillet over medium high heat, a few minutes per side. Season with salt to taste, remove from heat and keep warm.*

5. *Divide the rhubarb salsa onto heated plates and place the escalopes on top of the salsa. Top with the sauce, being careful to remove the whole peppercorns before serving. Use one long peppercorn per plate as a garnish, if you like.*

Pan-seared Escalope of Fresh Duck Foie Gras

Springtime Salad

of Duck Foie Gras, Asparagus, Viola Flowers, Honey Vinegar and Toasted Pine Nuts

This salad makes a spectacular first course for an elegant meal. Pairing a luxury product such as fresh foie gras with greens, flowers and spring vegetables may seem surprising, but the contrasting flavours are sublime. It's also very easy to make!

4 SERVINGS (AS AN APPETIZER)

INGREDIENTS

20 mL	natural cider vinegar	4 tsp
	salt, to taste	
15 mL	wildflower honey	1 tbsp
100 mL	sunflower oil or mild olive oil	⅜ cup
40 g	pine nuts	3 tbsp
200 g	foie gras "en torchon" (see page 161)	7 oz
16	green asparagus tips, blanched	16
200 g	mixed greens (chard leaves and tatsoy, or a mixture of your choice)	7 oz
15	viola flowers	15

Preparation

1. To prepare the vinaigrette, combine the cider vinegar, salt and honey, then add the sunflower or olive oil. Set aside.

2. Dry-roast the pine nuts in a small skillet and set aside.

3. Cut the foie gras into bite-size pieces.

Assembly

4. To serve, combine the vinaigrette, asparagus tips and greens. Arrange on chilled plates, then add the foie gras pieces, pine nuts and viola flowers.

Springtime Salad of Duck Foie Gras

Cannelloni Stuffed with Morels

and Duo du Paradis Cheese, Served with Sherry-flavoured Veal Jus and Goat's Milk Cheddar Tuiles

Here's a recipe inspired by Italian traditions but made with local products. Morels are quite expensive, but the recipe is just as delicious when made with other types of mushrooms. Duo du Paradis is a semi-firm white cheese with a washed rind, made from equal parts cow's and sheep's milk by Fromagerie l'Petit Train du Nord in Mont-Laurier.

6 SERVINGS

INGREDIENTS

300 g	spinach (2 bunches)	10 ½ oz
200 g	Duo du Paradis cheese, grated	7 oz
200 g	ricotta cheese	7 oz
1	egg	1
200 g	fresh morels, cut into pieces	7 oz
60 g	butter	1 ¾ oz
3	shallots, minced	3
	salt, to taste	
	nutmeg	
200 g	fresh pasta dough (see page 19)	7 oz
20 mL	sherry vinegar	4 tsp
100 mL	sherry	⅜ cup
500 mL	veal stock (see page 18)	2 cups
50 g	dried morels	1 ¾ oz
80 g	goat's milk cheddar, grated	3 oz
18	chive flowers	18

Preparation

1. The cannelloni may be prepared in advance. For the cannelloni filling, wash and blanch the spinach. Cool, drain and chop coarsely. Place in a bowl and add the Duo du Paradis cheese, ricotta and egg. Combine, then set aside.

2. In a small skillet, sauté the fresh morels in a little butter. Add ⅔ of the sliced shallots and cook for another 2 minutes. Let cool.

3. Combine the morels with the spinach mixture and mix well, using a fork. Season with salt to taste and sprinkle with nutmeg. Refrigerate.

4. Using a small pasta machine, roll the dough into 10-cm (4-in.) squares. Cook in salted boiling water for 1 minute or until they float to the surface. Drain and dry on clean towels.

5. Mound a little filling on each square; roll into cannelloni and place in a small, shallow buttered dish. Set aside.

6. In a saucepan, melt a little butter over high heat. Brown the remaining shallots, then deglaze the pan with the sherry vinegar. Add the sherry and 400 mL (1 ⅝ cups) of the veal stock. Add the dried morels and reduce over medium heat. Strain the sauce, season to taste and set aside.

7. Goat's Milk Cheddar Tuiles (see recipe on page 19).

Assembly

8. Preheat the oven to 190°C (375°F). Pour the remaining 100 mL (⅜ cup) of veal stock into the baking dish containing the cannelloni. Bake uncovered for about 15 minutes.

9. Heat the sauce and add the remaining butter and half of the chive flowers.

10. Arrange 2 cannelloni on each heated plate and surround with the sauce. Place a goat cheddar tuile on each plate and sprinkle the dishes with the remaining chive flowers.

Cannelloni Stuffed with Morels

Arctic Char

Mashed Potatoes and Oyster Mushrooms, Served with Frothy Olive Oil Sauce

Arctic char is a delicious freshwater fish that belongs to the Salmonidae family, like its cousin, the trout. It has delicate, mouth-watering flesh and smooth, shiny skin speckled with red.

4 SERVINGS

INGREDIENTS

1	shallot, minced	1
100 mL	extra-virgin olive oil	⅜ cup
175 mL	white wine	⅝ cup
200 mL	fish stock (see page 19)	¾ cup
15 mL	chopped fresh ginger	1 tbsp
50 mL	35% cream	3 tbsp
8	Ratte fingerling potatoes	4
	or	
2	Yukon Gold potatoes	2
1	green onion, minced	1
200 g	Arctic char fillets (50 g per serving)	7 oz
100 g	oyster mushrooms	3 ½ oz
50 mL	skim milk	3 tbsp

Preparation

1. *Sweat the shallot in a little olive oil. Deglaze with the white wine and add the fish stock. Add 8 mL (½ tbsp) of the ginger and the cream. Reduce, season with salt to taste and strain. Set the sauce aside.*

2. *Bake potatoes in a 200ºC (400ºF) oven until tender; a knife inserted should come out easily. While the potatoes are still hot, remove peels and use a fork to mash into a coarse purée, adding the green onions and 50 mL (3 tbsp) of the olive oil. Season with salt to taste and keep warm.*

3. *Place the Arctic char skin-side down in a hot skillet with a little olive oil and cook over medium heat for about 5 minutes, or until still rosy and about to flake. Season with salt. Do not overcook.*

4. *In the meantime, cook the oyster mushrooms in a little olive oil. Season with the salt and remaining ginger.*

Assembly

5. *Spoon the mashed potatoes and mushrooms onto heated plates, setting the char on top. Reheat the sauce, remove from heat, add the milk, and froth with a hand mixer. Pour over the fish.*

Arctic Char

**ANNE DESJARDINS
COOKS AT
L'EAU À LA BOUCHE**
THE SEASONAL CUISINE
OF QUEBEC

PAGE 45

Pan-fried Cod Fillet
Served on a Bed of Green and White Asparagus with Creamy Olive Oil Emulsion

This light, tasty spring dish can be served as a first course, or by doubling the quantities, as a main course. If white asparagus is not available, just double the amount of green asparagus. I make this recipe with cod, but my son Emmanuel prefers it with monkfish. You can use any firm-fleshed fish you like.

4 SERVINGS

INGREDIENTS

12 stalks	fresh green asparagus	12 stalks
8 stalks	fresh white asparagus	8 stalks
	juices of ½ lime, ½ orange and ½ grapefruit	
30 mL	Pernod	2 tbsp
100 mL	35% cream	⅜ cup
100 mL	extra-virgin olive oil	⅜ cup
	salt, to taste	
	Tabasco sauce	
	fresh tarragon sprigs	
4	cod fillets, 100 g (3 ½ oz) each	4
	zest of ½ lime, ½ orange and ½ grapefruit	

Preparation

1. Peel and trim the asparagus, then cut the stalks to an equal length. Blanch, cool and set aside.

2. In a small saucepan, bring the citrus juices, Pernod and cream to a boil and continue to boil for 2 minutes. Add 100 mL (⅜ cup) olive oil and season with salt to taste. Add a few drops of Tabasco and a few fresh tarragon leaves. Keep warm.

3. Heat a skillet and cook the cod fillets in a little olive oil for a few minutes per side. Sprinkle with some of the zest and tarragon leaves.

4. At the same time, in a small skillet, reheat the asparagus in a little olive oil. Season with salt and sprinkle with some more zest and tarragon leaves.

Assembly

5. On heated plates, arrange the asparagus stalks side by side, alternating white and green, to form a mat, and place the cod fillets on top. Top with the sauce. Garnish with zest and tarragon leaves.

Pan-fried Cod Fillet

Roasted Guinea Fowl Supreme

Braised Guinea Fowl Leg, Potatoes, Wild and Cultivated Mushrooms and Sherry Sauce

 Quebec breeders have only recently started raising guinea fowl but I've quickly adopted this bird, which I appreciate for its fine, tender flesh.

4 SERVINGS

INGREDIENTS

1	guinea fowl	1
3	pink shallots, peeled and halved	3
2	whole garlic cloves, peeled	2
1 bunch	fresh thyme	1 bunch
3	cloves	3
5	juniper berries	5
	sherry vinegar	
300 mL	sherry	1 ¼ cups
250 mL	mirepoix (1 carrot, 1 stalk celery and ½ leek, finely diced)	1 cup
	salt, to taste	
5	large Yukon Gold potatoes	5
200 g	unsalted butter	7 oz
500 g	mixed mushrooms (white, shiitake, morels)	1 ⅛ lb
50 mL	olive oil	3 tbsp
3	green onions, chopped	3
	butter	

Preparation

1. Remove the legs from the guinea fowl and place them in an oven-proof pot with a tight-fitting lid. Add the shallots, garlic cloves, a few thyme sprigs, the spices and a few drops of vinegar, then the sherry, mirepoix and some salt. Braise in the oven at 135°C (275°F), for 2 ½ hours.

2. Debone the breasts, keeping the skin and wings on. Refrigerate.

3. When the legs are done, debone the meat and keep warm. Strain the cooking juices and set aside.

4. Bake the potatoes in a 200°C (400°F) oven until tender; when pierced with a knife, it comes out easily. Peel and mash the potatoes while they're still hot. Put them through a food mill or ricer for a smooth consistency. Add butter. Season with salt to taste and keep warm.

5. Sauté the mushrooms in olive oil and season with salt. When done, add the chopped green onions. Drain and keep warm.

6. In a heavy skillet, cook the guinea fowl breasts in butter over medium heat. Season with salt. When three-quarters done, add the cooking juices from step 3 and cook over low heat until done. Crumble a little fresh thyme over the breasts.

Assembly

7. On heated plates, position the braised leg meat and mushrooms in 7.5-cm (3-in.) round moulds. Top with the mashed potatoes. Remove the rings. Cut each of the breasts into six thick slices, and place 3 on each plate. Season the sauce with salt, add a drop of sherry vinegar and butter, and spoon over. Garnish with thyme sprigs.

Roasted Guinea Fowl Supreme

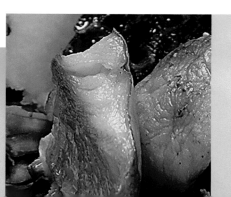

Pork Prepared Two Ways

Pan-seared Tenderloin and Braised Shoulder, with Traditional Quebec Spices, Potatoes and Pan Jus

I developed this recipe during one of my trips abroad as a guest chef, wanting to present a contemporary dish inspired by traditional Quebec cuisine. The choice of pork, the traditional mixture of spices, and the hearty preparation relying on root vegetables make it very much a Quebec dish. Using two different cuts of the best-quality pork, high-quality red wine and olive oil and a careful touch, it can be as dressy a dish as you like. The shoulder is braised, the tenderloin is cooked just before serving and the vegetables are prepared separately.

8 SERVINGS

INGREDIENTS

1	small pork shoulder, bone in	1
3	onions	3
1	garlic bulb	1
250 mL	red wine	1 cup
	fresh thyme sprigs	
10 mL	mixed ground spices (clove, nutmeg, allspice)	2 tsp
	salt, to taste	
1	large carrot, cut into sticks and then diagonally sliced	1
1	small parsnip, cut into sticks and then diagonally sliced	1
1	small celeriac, cut into sticks and then diagonally sliced	1
1	parsley root, cut into sticks and then diagonally sliced	1
500 g	Yukon Gold potatoes (about 6)	1 ⅛ lb
500 g	pork tenderloin (about 60 g [2 oz] per serving)	1 ⅛ lb
	olive oil	
150 g	unsalted butter	5 ⅓ oz

Preparation

1. *Place the pork shoulder in an enamelled cast iron pot (or any non-reactive heavy pot with a lid) with the onions, garlic and red wine. Add a few thyme leaves and 5 mL (1 tsp) of the spice mixture. Season generously with salt. Cover and braise in a very low-temperature oven (120°C [250°F]), for 5 ½ hours.*

2. *In the meantime, blanch the sliced root vegetables and refrigerate.*

3. *When the shoulder is done, remove from the pot and debone. Keep the meat warm. Strain half of the cooking juices into a small saucepan and reduce to a saucy consistency. Set aside the other half of the juices to be used to cook the potatoes. Correct the seasoning.*

4. *Peel and quarter the potatoes. Cook the potatoes in the reserved cooking juices and set aside.*

Assembly

5. *Shortly before serving, preheat the oven to 205°C (400°F). Slice the pork tenderloin into 4.25-cm (1 ¾-in.) medallions. In a skillet, sear them in a little olive oil over high heat. Sprinkle with the remaining spice mixture, remove from the skillet and place on a baking sheet in the oven for 5 minutes. Remove and let rest, tented with aluminum foil.*

6. *In a frying pan, sauté the blanched vegetables in a little olive oil over high heat. Season with salt. Use a fork to mash the potatoes with a little butter. Season with salt and thyme.*

7. *Serve on large heated plates, allotting 80 g (or a serving spoonful) of braised shoulder and a medallion of tenderloin per person. Accompany with the mashed potatoes and the mixture of root vegetables. Allow your inspiration and the occasion to dictate the presentation. Drizzle with the pan jus and garnish with a thyme sprig and/or a sprinkle of spices on the rim of the plate.*

Pork Prepared Two Ways

Laracam Cheese
with Cumin-flavoured Apple Jelly

Martin Guilbault and his family, from Fromagerie du Champ à la Meule in Lanaudière, make a creamy, washed-rind cheese with a fairly sharp taste called Laracam. Let the cheese stand at room temperature for a few hours before serving.

Apples from the orchards in St.-Joseph-du-Lac and Oka are still very good at this time of year. The fresh apple jelly is subtly flavoured with cumin, and should be made several hours in advance so it has time to set. Toasted rye bread makes a delicious accompaniment to this dish.

4 SERVINGS

INGREDIENTS

250 mL	fresh apple juice (if possible, juice two large Empire apples)	1 cup
	cumin seeds	
	fresh lemon juice	
1 pinch	salt	1 pinch
1 pinch	granulated sugar	1 pinch
3 leaves (6 g)	gelatin, soaked in cold water, squeezed dry	3 leaves (¾ pkg)
400 g	Laracam cheese	14 oz
	rye bread	

Preparation

1. To make the jelly, bring the apple juice, cumin seeds, lemon juice, salt and sugar to a boil and let steep for 2 minutes. Dissolve the softened gelatin in the apple juice. Pour through a fine strainer into a square non-reactive container or small, deep dish so that the liquid is at least 1 cm (½ in.) deep. Let cool until set. Once at room temperature, it should be refrigerated until needed.

Assembly

2. To serve, cut the jelly into large cubes. Toast the rye bread and cut it into thin slices. Serve both alongside the cheese.

Laracam Cheese

Warm Maple Butter Pound Cake

Maple Ice Cream and Rhubarb Compote with Aged Balsamic Vinegar and Indonesian Long Pepper

I love this pound cake. It recalls traditional recipes in which rhubarb, flavoured with balsamic vinegar and spiced with pepper, counterbalances the very sweet maple taste.

Make the cake centres, compote and ice cream a day ahead.

POUND CAKE FOR 10 SMALL (100 mL [3 OZ]) RAMEKINS

INGREDIENTS

POUND CAKE

250 g	maple butter	9 oz
75 g	white chocolate	2 ⅔ oz
5	large eggs, separated	5
150 g	granulated sugar	5 ⅓ oz
150 g	unsalted butter, softened	5 ⅓ oz
150 g	all-purpose flour	5 ⅓ oz
15 mL	butter, softened	1 tbsp

RHUBARB COMPOTE

500 g	rhubarb (about 6 stalks)	1 ⅛ lb
500 g	granulated sugar	1 ⅛ lb
3	whole long pepper peppercorns	3
100 mL	balsamic vinegar (aged minimum ten years)	⅜ cup

MAPLE ICE CREAM

500 mL	35% cream	2 cups
270 mL	maple syrup	1 ⅛ cup

Preparation

1. To make the maple centres for the individual pound cakes, melt the maple butter and white chocolate in a double boiler and cool partially, until thick enough to pipe or shape. Using a piping bag or spoon, divide into 10 small portions on a baking tray lined with parchment paper. Set aside in a cool place, or freeze.

2. Using a mixer, beat the egg yolks and the sugar (reserving 30 mL [2 tbsp] of the sugar). Add the 150 g (5 ⅓ oz) of softened unsalted butter, and beat well. Gradually add the flour. In a separate bowl, beat the egg whites with the 30 mL (2 tbsp) of sugar until stiff. Fold into the egg yolk mixture.

3. Grease the ramekins with softened butter. Fill each ramekin halfway with the batter. Place a portion of the maple butter–white chocolate mixture in each ramekin and top with the remaining batter. Place in the freezer for 1 day.

4. A half-hour before serving, bake the ramekins in the oven at 190°C (375°F) for 15 minutes.

5. For the rhubarb compote, cut the rhubarb into small pieces, place in a bowl and add 250 g (9 oz) sugar. Cover and refrigerate.

6. After a few hours, drain off the liquid that the rhubarb has released. Place half of the liquid in a saucepan, along with 250 g (9 oz) sugar and the pepper. Reduce until it forms a caramel, or reaches 134°C (273°F). Add the balsamic vinegar to stop the cooking process.

7. Add the warm caramel to the rhubarb pieces, along with some of the remaining rhubarb liquid, if needed, to make a juicy compote.

8. Place the cream and maple syrup in an ice cream maker and follow the manufacturer's instructions. Place in the freezer.

Assembly

9. Place each warm cake on a plate with a spoonful of the compote and a scoop of ice cream. Drizzle some of the caramel from the rhubarb compote over the cakes.

Warm Maple Butter Pound Cake

summer

When summer arrives at long last, it is short but very intense. In the sweltering heat of July, with temperatures approaching forty degrees Celsius and high humidity, flowers, fruits and vegetables grow incredibly fast. Everywhere, the countryside is lovely to behold, and at the restaurant, our business hits full swing.

acationers and tourists are enjoying their holidays, the reservation book is full and we are as busy as bees, turning outstanding local products into dishes that will delight our guests. A steady stream of producers visits L'Eau à la Bouche, bringing juicy, bright-red raspberries and freshly picked chanterelles. There's always Terry Hussey from Insalada in Prévost, who brings us baskets of early vegetables and various greens, and Pierre arriving from his rounds in St.-Joseph-du-Lac, with serviceberries, currants, cherries and black raspberries. Beginning in early August, the Bourassa country market has wonderful wild blueberries from the Upper Laurentians.

Honey is available year-round, of course, but the honey of summer is the most fragrant, since our northern location means the flowering season is brief and intense. I have a weakness for honey from the Desrochers farm near Ferme-Neuve in the Upper Laurentians, a wild region untainted by industrial pollution. Their bees produce a natural, fragrant honey that is sold unpasteurized. I am also very fond of the wild mint honey skillfully harvested by Anicet Desrochers, as well as their spring wildflower honey. And I am in awe of the consummate skill that goes into producing the celebrated Cuvée du Diable mead that Claude and Marie-Claude Desrochers age in oak casks — it's nothing short of a marvel.

My own garden yields edible flowers such as day lilies (which taste like wild honey), peppery nasturtiums, tangy monarda (bee balm) and borage. It's also the high season for aromatic herbs such as chives, basil, tarragon, coriander, sage and mint.

Our foragers and collectors bring us shoots of milkweed, wild purslane, mustard and stonecrop. The shores of the St. Lawrence yield a maritime mesclun of sea-rocket leaves (*Cakile edentula*), tender sprigs of salicornia (*Salicornia europaea*), saline plantain (*Plantago eripoda*) and sandwort (*Arenaria*).

Our market gardeners provide us with a dazzling variety of organic produce: two-colour radishes, heirloom tomatoes, cucumber, corn, zucchini, pattypan squash, multi-coloured carrots in different shapes and sizes, mizuna and chrysanthemum lettuce, tatsoy, orach and pink, yellow and white beets.

Mushroom collectors bring us chanterelles, fairy ring mushrooms (*Marasmius*) and milkcap (*Lactaria*). The St. Lawrence River offers up urchins, sturgeon, eel and crayfish, and our lakes abound with walleye, whitefish and trout. From local breeders, we receive fresh foie gras, quail, guinea fowl and baby goat. The list could go on and on...

PRECEDING PAGES: MY VAGABOND OF THE WOODS, FRANÇOIS BROUILLARD

RIGHT: SOME OF THE FLOWERS IN THE GARDEN AT L'EAU À LA BOUCHE

Organic Tomato Gazpacho
with Scallop Tartare, Coriander, Pepper Confetti and Yellow Tomato Granita

 Summer brings hot sunny weather, and that means flavourful, juicy tomatoes from our local growers. I've taken the traditional recipe for this chilled soup from Spain and put my own spin on it!

Inspired by summer's abundance, experiment with the different varieties of tomatoes in your garden, in your neighbour's garden or those available from local growers. Or perhaps try this recipe with the yellow tomato variety or the Zebra. And if scallops aren't available, the tartare can also be made with tuna.

6 SERVINGS

INGREDIENTS

GAZPACHO

5	large organic tomatoes	5
2	bell peppers, seeded and coarsely chopped (reserve 15 mL [1 tbsp] finely diced pepper for garnish)	2
1	cucumber, peeled and cut into large chunks	1
1	shallot	1
30 mL	cider vinegar **or** sherry vinegar	2 tbsp
	juice and zest of 1 lime	
75 mL	extra-virgin olive oil	5 tbsp
60 mL	chopped fresh coriander	4 tbsp
	salt, to taste	
	Tabasco sauce	

YELLOW TOMATO GRANITA

250 mL	fresh organic tomato juice	1 cup
	lime juice	
5 mL	sugar	1 tsp
	salt, to taste	
	Tabasco sauce	
	gazpacho (reserved from step 1)	

SCALLOP TARTARE

180 g	raw scallops, well cleaned, muscle removed	6 ⅓ oz
15 mL	lime juice	1 tbsp
15 mL	olive oil	1 tbsp
5 mL	minced green onion	1 tsp
	salt, to taste	
	lime zest	
	Tabasco sauce	

Preparation

1. Blanch and peel the tomatoes. Cut into pieces and purée in the blender. Strain and set aside 250 mL (1 cup) of the juice.

2. Return the rest of the tomato juice to the blender, along with the other ingredients for the gazpacho. Blend well and correct the seasoning as necessary. Refrigerate.

3. Add the ingredients for the granita recipe to the juice reserved in step 1. Pour into a shallow pan and freeze for at least 4 hours.

Assembly

4. An hour before serving, cut the scallops into small cubes. Combine with the other tartare ingredients and refrigerate.

5. To serve, pour the gazpacho into chilled soup plates, add 2 spoonfuls of scallop tartare to the centre and top with a little diced pepper and chopped coriander. Break up the tomato granita into shards with a fork and place a forkful or a nice quenelle on top of the scallops.

Organic Tomato Gazpacho

Smoked Duck Salad
with Julienned Yellow Beets, Purslane and Wild Blackberries

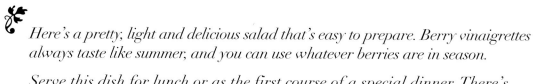 *Here's a pretty, light and delicious salad that's easy to prepare. Berry vinaigrettes always taste like summer, and you can use whatever berries are in season.*

Serve this dish for lunch or as the first course of a special dinner. There's nothing like the fresh taste of berries to whet the appetite.

4 SERVINGS

INGREDIENTS

	salt, to taste	
3 mL	Dijon mustard	½ tsp
200 g	wild blackberries	7 oz
30 mL	natural cider vinegar	2 tbsp
100 mL	extra-virgin olive oil	⅜ cup
1	smoked duck breast (available at some delicatessens and butcher shops)	1
2	large yellow beets, cooked and peeled	2
500 g	purslane (or lamb's lettuce, or baby spinach)	1 ⅛ lb

Preparation

1. *Combine mustard, salt, 5 blackberries, cider vinegar and olive oil in a blender and process until smooth. Set aside.*

2. *Remove the fat from the duck breast and slice the meat thinly. Set aside.*

3. *Cut the 2 beets into julienne strips and combine with half the vinaigrette.*

Assembly

4. *Arrange the julienned beets in the centres of chilled plates and surround with the smoked duck breast. Combine the purslane with the remaining vinaigrette and arrange it around each plate. Garnish with the remaining blackberries (and flowers from the garden, if you wish).*

Smoked Duck Salad

**ANNE DESJARDINS
COOKS AT
L'EAU À LA BOUCHE**
THE SEASONAL CUISINE
OF QUEBEC

PAGE 71

Mild Garlic Crème Brûlée

with a Garden and Field Vegetable Medley, Flower Petals and Hazelnut Oil

This recipe is a favourite with my customers. I call it crème brûlée, but in classic cuisine the correct term would be royale. Creamy and flavoured with garlic made mild by cooking, it's a wonderful accompaniment for fresh summer vegetables.

CRÈME BRÛLÉE FOR 6 SMALL (100 mL [3 oz]) RAMEKINS

INGREDIENTS

VINAIGRETTE

15 g	salt	½ oz
60 mL	natural cider vinegar	4 tbsp
200 mL	hazelnut oil	¾ cup
5 mL	toasted sesame oil	1 tsp
25	garlic cloves, peeled and germ centre removed	25
250 mL	35% cream	1 cup
90 mL	whole milk	6 tbsp
3	egg yolks	3
1	egg	1
1 pinch	freshly grated nutmeg	1 pinch
150 g	freshly grated goat's milk cheddar	5 ⅓ oz
500 g	assortment of vegetables, blanched (for example, 6 baby carrots with tops, 6 miniature beets, 6 stalks asparagus, 6 miniature zucchini, 6 radishes)	1 ⅛ lb
60 mL	edible flower petals from the garden (for example, borage, calendula, viola)	¼ cup

Preparation

1. To prepare the vinaigrette, dissolve the salt in the cider vinegar, then add the hazelnut oil and toasted sesame oil. Blend well and set aside.

2. Preheat the oven to 95°C (200°F).

3. Blanch the garlic cloves for 2 minutes in a small amount of boiling water. Drain. Boil more water and boil the garlic cloves until they are tender. Drain again.

4. Place the garlic cloves, cream, milk, egg yolks, egg and nutmeg in a blender. Blend well, without overmixing.

5. Taste and correct the seasoning as required.

6. Pour into ovenproof ramekins. Place the ramekins on a baking sheet. Bake for about 30 minutes until set. They should still be slightly wobbly in the centre but moving as a cohesive mass.

7. Remove from the oven and let cool.

Assembly

8. Just before serving, sprinkle the ramekins with the grated goat's milk cheddar and place under the broiler to grill lightly.

9. Combine the vegetables and the vinaigrette. Place a ramekin in the centre of each plate and surround with vegetables. Garnish with flower petals.

Mild Garlic Crème Brûlée

Gingered Trout Fillet
with Mead–Carrot Juice Reduction

Although trout has always been part of our culinary tradition, the sale of wild trout is now prohibited. Fortunately, Quebec has many fish farmers who raise excellent trout. The fine flesh of this fish is a perfect match for the spiced carrot juice.

I started making this recipe in the 1980s, after I attended a seminar where I sampled pike-perch in carrot juice, created by French chef Gérard Vié. I then tried my hand at this recipe, using products from my own region.

4 SERVINGS

INGREDIENTS

4	carrots, julienned	4
110 g	unsalted butter	4 oz
4	trout fillets, 80 g (3 oz) each	4
	salt, to taste	
	zest and juice of 1 lemon	
30 mL	freshly grated ginger	2 tbsp
4	carrots, to yield 250 mL (1 cup) juice (or ready-made carrot juice)	4
1	shallot, minced	1
200 mL	Cuvée du Diable mead (or floral white wine)	¾ cup

Preparation

1. *Blanch the julienned carrots and set aside.*

2. *Preheat the oven to 205°C (400°F). Melt half the butter and baste the trout fillets with it. Sprinkle with salt, lemon zest and half the grated ginger. Roll the trout fillet into a spiral and place in a deep buttered dish. Refrigerate.*

3. *Using a juicer, juice the carrots to obtain 250 mL (1 cup) juice (or use ready-made carrot juice).*

4. *In a small saucepan, melt a little butter and cook the shallot until golden brown. Add the remaining grated ginger, 15 mL (1 tbsp) lemon juice and mead. Reduce for 2 minutes over low heat, then add the carrot juice and simmer to reduce by half. Strain. Add salt if needed and set aside.*

Assembly

5. *Just before serving, bake the trout fillets for about 5 minutes, or until the flesh is opaque but still pink in the centre.*

6. *Heat the reduction; gently stir in 50 g (1 ¾ oz) butter.*

7. *Sauté the vegetables with a little butter and 5 mL (1 tsp) grated ginger. Add salt and arrange a small pile of carrots on each heated plate.*

8. *Place the spirals of trout on the vegetables and top with reduction. Garnish.*

Gingered Trout Fillet

Gulf of St. Lawrence Scallops

Roasted on One Side, Served with Summer Tomatoes and Basil, Salicornia and Creamy Olive Oil Emulsion

 This recipe has become a classic at L'Eau à la Bouche, where I've been serving it for nearly 20 years. Salicornia, also called marsh samphire, glasswort (Salicornia europaea) or sea asparagus, grows in the salt marshes of the St. Lawrence River and is a perfect complement to fish and seafood. Double the quantities for a main dish.

6 SERVINGS

INGREDIENTS

TOMATOES

1	small onion, chopped	1
1	garlic clove, peeled and chopped	1
50 mL	virgin olive oil	3 tbsp
200 mL	tomatoes, cored, cut into chunks and drained	¾ cup
	Tabasco sauce	
	salt, to taste	

ROASTED SCALLOPS

5 mL	extra-virgin olive oil	1 tsp
18	large fresh scallops (3 per person)	18
	salt, to taste	
8	fresh basil leaves, finely chopped	8
100 g	salicornia, trimmed and blanched	3 ½ oz
180 mL	warm creamy olive oil emulsion (see page 21)	¾ cup

Preparation

1. *Cook the onion and garlic in the olive oil until golden brown. Add the drained tomatoes. Cook over low heat for 5 minutes; taste and season with Tabasco and salt. Set aside.*

Assembly

2. *In a nonstick or heavy stainless steel skillet, heat 5 mL (1 tsp) olive oil and sear the scallops over high heat, one side only. Cook until the scallops are opaque halfway through and sprinkle with salt.*

3. *In the meantime, add half the basil to the tomatoes and reheat the tomato mixture.*

4. *Reheat the salicornia by sautéing it quickly in a little olive oil.*

5. *Bring the creamy olive oil emulsion to a boil for 30 seconds and add the remaining basil at the last minute.*

6. *Arrange the tomatoes and salicornia in the centre of heated plates. Place 3 scallops around them and drizzle the emulsion around the edge.*

**ANNE DESJARDINS
COOKS AT
L'EAU À LA BOUCHE**
THE SEASONAL CUISINE
OF QUEBEC

PAGE 80

*Gulf of St. Lawrence
Scallops*

Small Eggplants
Stuffed with Chanterelles, Cherry Tomatoes, Green Onions, Basil and Veal Reduction

Here's a recipe that takes its inspiration from local produce available in August: eggplants, tomatoes, wild mushrooms and herbs. The freshness and colours of the ingredients make this dish a pleasure to prepare.

To make the dish more substantial, add a little cheese. Duo du Paradis, a semi-firm washed rind cheese from Mont-Laurier, made with cow's and sheep's milk, is an excellent choice.

4 SERVINGS

INGREDIENTS

4	small eggplants, about 11 cm (4 ⅓ in.) each	4
75 mL	extra-virgin olive oil	5 tbsp
20	cherry tomatoes	20
200 g	chanterelles	7 oz
15 mL	balsamic vinegar	1 tbsp
100 mL	red wine	⅜ cup
250 mL	veal stock (see page 18)	1 cup
4	green onions, minced	4
	fresh basil leaves, chopped	
	salt, to taste	
	Tabasco sauce	

Preparation

1. *Preheat the oven to 205°C (400°F). Cut the eggplants in half and brush the cut surfaces with olive oil. Place on a baking sheet cut-sides down and bake in the oven for about 20 minutes. Let cool and scoop out the flesh of the eggplants using a small knife and a spoon. Set aside the flesh and the eggplant shells separately.*
2. *Cut the tomatoes in half (they do not need to be cored) and set aside. Clean the chanterelles and cut them in half if they are too large. Set aside.*
3. *In a small saucepan, reduce the balsamic vinegar and red wine by simmering over low heat. Add the veal stock, reduce by half, correct the seasoning and set aside.*
4. *Place the eggplant shells cut-sides up in the oven at 150°C (300°F) for 5 minutes to reheat and crisp up.*
5. *In a skillet, sauté the chanterelles in a little olive oil for a few minutes. Add the tomatoes and the eggplant flesh. Cook for a few minutes, then add the green onions and basil. Add salt and a few drops of Tabasco to taste.*

Assembly

6. *Remove the eggplant shells from the oven and place on heated plates. Fill with the warm vegetable mixture. Pour the sauce over the vegetables. Garnish with basil.*

Small Eggplants

Goat-cheese Ravioli
with Sautéed Wild Mushrooms and Veal Jus

I have a weakness for ravioli. At the restaurant, I vary my ravioli recipes with the seasons. This one is particularly rich in flavour. It must be prepared in stages: the pasta dough and the ravioli must be made first, and the other steps completed at the last minute.

The ravioli filling contains a little gelatin, so that it can be piped when cold, but it is liquid when hot, giving it a delicious melt-in-your-mouth texture.

6 SERVINGS (AS AN APPETIZER)

INGREDIENTS

GOAT-CHEESE FILLING FOR RAVIOLI

1	shallot, minced	1
15 mL	extra-virgin olive oil	1 tbsp
60 mL	white wine	4 tbsp
100 g	fresh goat cheese	3 ½ oz
50 mL	35% cream	3 tbsp
2 leaves (4 g)	gelatin, soaked in cold water, squeezed dry	2 leaves (½ pkg)
	salt, to taste	
	Tabasco sauce	
½ recipe	fresh pasta dough (see page 19)	½ recipe
1	egg, beaten	1

MUSHROOMS

300 g	fresh wild mushrooms (or oyster mushrooms or shiitakes)	10 ½ oz
30 mL	extra-virgin olive oil	2 tbsp
	salt, to taste	
2	green onions, minced	2
60 mL	sherry	4 tbsp
300 mL	veal stock (see page 18)	1 ¼ cups
15 mL	butter	1 tbsp

Preparation

1. Sweat the shallot in a little olive oil. Add the white wine and cook until almost all the wine has evaporated. Remove from heat and add the goat cheese.

2. Bring the cream to a boil, add the softened gelatin and stir into the goat cheese mixture. Season with salt and add a few drops of Tabasco. Set aside.

3. Make the ravioli by rolling out the dough into thin strips 5 cm (2 in.) wide, and place each strip on a lightly floured surface. Keep the dough moist while you work by covering the unused portions with plastic wrap or a damp towel. On half of the dough strips, place 15 mL (1 tbsp) filling at intervals of 4 cm (1 ½ in.). Brush beaten egg around the filling mounds and top with another strip of dough. Make sure to seal the ravioli by gently pressing the dough around the filling, eliminating any air bubbles in the process. Cut the dough into ravioli shapes with a knife or a metal ring. Place on a lightly floured surface and refrigerate or freeze. If frozen, do not thaw the ravioli before cooking them.

Assembly

4. Sauté the mushrooms in the olive oil, then add salt and the green onion. Transfer to a small dish and keep warm. Deglaze the skillet with the sherry and veal stock. Simmer to reduce by half and add the butter. Season with salt to taste and set aside.

5. At the same time, bring salted water to a rolling boil in a heavy-bottomed pot. Cook the ravioli in the boiling water (1 to 2 minutes will suffice, since the pasta is fresh). Allow a few more minutes if the pasta is frozen. Drain carefully, as the ravioli are quite fragile.

6. Place a layer of mushrooms on each heated plate. Add 3 ravioli per plate and top with the sauce.

Goat-cheese Ravioli

Walleye Fillets with St. Lawrence Crayfish
Summer Vegetable Medley and Basil

In this summery recipe, walleye, a freshwater fish with delicate flesh, is combined with crayfish, which not that long ago were scorned by St. Lawrence fishermen. Amateur cooks will enjoy preparing this easy recipe.

4 SERVINGS

INGREDIENTS

2	garlic cloves, minced	2
4	green onions, minced	4
	zest and juice of 1 orange	
	extra-virgin olive oil	
200 mL	white vermouth	¾ cup
300 mL	water	1 ¼ cups
	salt, to taste	
	Tabasco sauce	
12	live crayfish	12
4	walleye fillets, 175 g (6 oz) each	4
	fresh basil leaves, chopped	
1	red pepper, finely diced	1
8	miniature pattypan squash, diced	8
	or	
1	zucchini, diced	1

Preparation

1. Cook the garlic, half the green onions, and half the orange zest in olive oil. Add the orange juice, white vermouth and water. Season with salt and a few drops of Tabasco. Bring to a boil.

2. Cook the crayfish by immersing them in the boiling liquid for about 3 minutes. Do not overcook. When they are just starting to turn red, remove them from the pot.

3. Separate the tails from the crayfish bodies. Set aside the tails and return the bodies to the liquid. Simmer to reduce the bouillon by half. Strain the bouillon and set aside. Keep 4 crayfish heads for garnish and discard the rest.

Assembly

4. Preheat the oven to 65°C (150°F).

5. On the stove, heat a little olive oil in a heavy-bottomed or nonstick skillet. Cook the walleye fillets for a few minutes on each side over medium heat and remove from the skillet. Place in an ovenproof dish. Season with salt and sprinkle with zest and basil. Keep warm in the oven.

6. In the same skillet, sauté the diced vegetables, the other half of the green onions and crayfish tails in a little olive oil. Remove from the skillet and place with the walleye fillets in the oven.

7. Deglaze the skillet with the crayfish bouillon. Simmer to reduce to a sauce consistency and season with salt, Tabasco and fresh basil.

8. Divide the vegetables and crayfish between 4 heated plates, and place the walleye fillets on top. Pour the sauce over each fillet and garnish with crayfish heads.

Walleye Fillets with St. Lawrence Crayfish

ANNE DESJARDINS COOKS AT L'EAU À LA BOUCHE
THE SEASONAL CUISINE OF QUEBEC

Atlantic Halibut Fillets
Maritime Herbs and Chanterelles, and Mushroom Ginger Froth

Mushrooms, ginger and fish: this dish combines contrasting flavours that are mild yet distinctive.

Be sure to use organic canola oil in this recipe (for example, Highwood Crossing canola oil from Alberta) since it is much more flavourful and nuttier-tasting than standard canola oil. Baby spinach and arugula, or even julienned baby zucchini, can be substituted for the orach and salicornia.

4 SERVINGS

INGREDIENTS

1	shallot, minced	1
	organic canola oil	
5 mL	natural cider vinegar	1tsp
150 mL	dry cider	⅝ cup
150 mL	water	⅝ cup
50 g	dried wild mushrooms	1 ¾ oz
30 mL	grated fresh ginger	2 tbsp
4	fresh Atlantic halibut fillets, 175 g (6 oz) each	4
	salt, to taste	
120 g	fresh chanterelles	4 ¼ oz
200 g	mixture of orach and salicornia (or substitute spinach and arugula)	7 oz
12	cherry tomatoes, quartered	12
150 mL	milk	⅝ cup

Preparation

1. Sweat the shallot in a little canola oil and deglaze with the vinegar and cider. Add the water and steep the wild mushrooms and 15 mL (1 tbsp) ginger in this liquid. Simmer until reduced by half. Strain the sauce and set aside.

Assembly

2. To serve, preheat the oven to 65°C (150°F). In a heavy-bottomed or nonstick skillet, cook the halibut fillets in a little canola oil a few minutes per side, over medium heat. Remove from the skillet and place in an ovenproof dish. Season with salt and keep warm in the oven.

3. In the same skillet, sauté the chanterelles in a little canola oil with some ginger and a pinch of salt. Remove from the pan and keep warm. Add the greens and tomatoes to the skillet and cook briefly. Season with salt to taste.

4. Heat the sauce, adding the milk. Taste and correct the seasoning; remove from heat. Using a hand mixer, whip the sauce until it is frothy. It should be warm, but not boiling hot, in order to froth properly.

5. Arrange the vegetables and chanterelles on heated plates. Place the halibut fillets on top and spoon the sauce over them.

Atlantic Halibut Fillets

Roasted Squab Supremes
with Cippolini Onions, and Pan Jus with St.-Joseph-du-Lac Berries

For some years, Bellechasse has been producing squab of outstanding quality. The reddish meat tastes like that of a wild bird with a mild, gamy poultry flavour. Squab must be cooked, preferably bone in, just until the meat is pink and still red at the bone in order to maintain its delicate flavour.

I like serving poultry with sweet and sour fruit or berry sauces. You can use blackberries, Montmorency cherries, raspberries, black currants, serviceberries, blueberries or any other variety you like.

4 SERVINGS

INGREDIENTS

4	fresh squabs, 375 g (13 oz) each	4
1	shallot, sliced	1
50 g	butter	5 ⅓ oz
4	juniper berries	4
200 g	berries	7 oz
	fresh thyme sprigs	
30 mL	balsamic vinegar	2 tbsp
125 mL	red wine	½ cup
250 mL	hearty poultry stock, made with squab bones and legs (see page 18)	1 cup
12	small new cippolini onions or other very mild small onions	12

Preparation

1. Debone the squabs, leaving the breast bones in and the skin and wings attached. Refrigerate the supremes. Make a stock using the carcasses and legs.

2. Cook the sliced shallot in a little butter with the juniper berries, half the berries and a few sprigs of thyme. Deglaze with the balsamic vinegar and red wine, then add the stock. Simmer until reduced by half. Strain and set the sauce aside, discarding the berries and thyme.

3. Cook the onions whole in a little butter over low heat. Season with salt and cook until caramelized. Set aside.

Assembly

4. Preheat the oven to 65°C (150°F).

5. To serve, cook the squab supremes (skin-side down) in a little butter, in a heavy skillet, over medium heat. Brown well, and then turn to cook the other side until the meat is rosy. Remove from the skillet, season with salt and place in the oven to keep warm.

6. Degrease the skillet, then add the sauce and the remaining berries. Add a little butter and salt to taste.

7. Remove the bones from the squab supremes, leaving the wing intact.

8. Arrange onions and 2 squab supremes on each heated plate and top with sauce. Decorate with thyme sprigs.

Roasted Squab Supremes

Rabbit Prepared Two Ways
Pan-seared and Braised, with Eggplants, Leeks and Tomatoes, and Pan Jus with Red Wine and Mild Garlic

A few years ago, I began preparing meats two different ways on the same menu. My customers appreciate it because it's a great way to discover new flavours and enjoy less popular cuts. Now, I almost always prepare meat two or more ways for the same dish, varying the recipes with the seasons.

8 SERVINGS

INGREDIENTS

2	leeks, trimmed and thinly sliced	2
200 g	pitted black olives	7 oz
1	stalk celery, diced	1
2	large tomatoes, quartered	2
3	bay leaves	3
12	large garlic cloves, peeled	12
2	rabbits, saddle deboned and legs bone in	2
30 mL	red wine vinegar	2 tbsp
375 mL	red wine	2 ½ cups
	sprigs of thyme and rosemary	
1	large eggplant, peeled, degorged (sliced and sprinkled with coarse salt; after a half-hour, pat dry), diced	1
100 mL	extra-virgin olive oil	⅜ cup
24	cherry tomatoes, halved	24
	salt, to taste	
	sea salt	

Preparation

1. Preheat the oven to 138°C (280°F).

2. Mix half the leek and half the olives with the celery, quartered tomatoes, bay leaves and 5 peeled garlic cloves in a braising pan.

3. Place the legs on top of the vegetables, then pour the wine vinegar and red wine over them. Crumble some thyme and rosemary on top and cover.

4. Bake in the oven for 2 hours. During the last half-hour, baste the legs with the cooking juices twice.

5. Remove from the oven. Strain the cooking juices, mashing the vegetables to extract all of their flavour. Skim the fat off the liquid, transfer to a saucepan and reduce by half. Set aside.

6. Debone the cooked legs and return the meat to the braising pan. Spoon 75 mL (5 tbsp) reduced cooking juices over the meat. Cover with aluminum foil and keep warm in the oven.

7. Sauté the eggplant and the remaining sliced leek in a little olive oil. Add the cherry tomatoes and cook for 5 minutes until the components come together but are still identifiable.

Assembly

8. To serve, pan-sear the rabbit saddles in a little olive oil in a heavy skillet, until brown on all sides. This will take about 5 minutes; be careful not to overcook. Season with salt. Set aside.

9. Heat the cooking juices over high heat until reduced by half. Correct the seasoning to taste.

10. Arrange the pieces of rabbit leg in the centres of heated plates. Slice the saddles and place them on top. Position the eggplant mixture beside the meat, then pour the cooking juices over the meat. Sprinkle the saddles with sea salt and garnish with sprigs of thyme and rosemary.

Rabbit Prepared Two Ways

Veal Trio

Pan-seared Fillet, Braised Cheeks and Sweetbreads, with Sherry Sauce and Baby Root Vegetables from the Lower Laurentians

Veal is a meat I like to prepare three different ways, as I love all the various cuts. This dish features different textures all subtly tied together by the cooking juices.

4 SERVINGS

INGREDIENTS

8	small young carrots	8
4	small young parsley roots	4
8	small young celery roots	8
12	small onions (cippolini if possible)	12
350 g	heart sweetbreads	12 ⅓ oz
2	veal cheeks	2
	butter	
	chopped parsley	
	fresh thyme sprigs	
30 mL	sherry vinegar	2 tbsp
100 mL	sherry	⅜ cup
100 mL	veal stock (see page 18)	⅜ cup
1	veal fillet, 300 g (10 ½ oz)	1
	or	
4	veal medallions, cut from the tenderloin, 75 g (2 ⅔ oz) each	4
	salt, to taste	
60 mL	35% cream	4 tbsp

Preparation

These first steps may be completed a day in advance and the food refrigerated overnight.

1. *Blanch, cool and set aside half of each of the root vegetables. Coarsely chop the remaining vegetables and set aside.*

2. *Prepare half the basic recipe for veal sweetbreads (see page 20), reserving the cooking juices.*

3. *Trim the cheeks. In a medium saucepan, brown them in a little butter. Add the chopped vegetables and some parsley and thyme. Deglaze with the vinegar and sherry. Add the veal stock and simmer over low heat for 2 to 2 ½ hours, or place in a 135°C (275°F) oven for 2 ½ hours, until the meat is tender and pulls apart easily*

4. *Remove the meat. Strain the cooking juices and set aside. Debone the meat and set aside.*

Assembly

5. *Pan-sear the veal fillet (or medallions) in a skillet over high heat for a few minutes each side. Season with salt and set aside.*

6. *Combine the cooking juices from both the sweetbreads and the veal cheeks and reduce slightly.*

7. *Add the sweetbreads and cheeks to the cooking juices. Correct the seasoning, add the 35% cream and a little butter.*

8. *In a skillet, sauté the blanched whole root vegetables in a little butter. Add salt and some parsley and thyme.*

9. *Arrange the three veal preparations together on heated plates, along with the root vegetables. Garnish with fresh thyme sprigs.*

Veal Trio

Renée's Wild Blueberry Cobbler
with Maple Blueberry Granita

This recipe was adapted from a number of different sources and inspired by summer's abundance of berries. My mother-in-law, Renée Audette, gave me the original recipe, which I have since modified several times.

The granita can also be served as a refreshing pause during a meal, or as a light dessert or a snack.

8 (200 mL [6 oz]) RAMEKINS OR OVENPROOF SOUP BOWLS

INGREDIENTS

BLUEBERRY MAPLE GRANITA

125 mL	puréed wild blueberries	½ cup
125 mL	maple syrup	½ cup
15 mL	lemon juice	1 tbsp
200 mL	Val Ambré maple liqueur	7 oz
8	day lily petals or mint leaves, for garnish	8

COBBLER

200 mL	maple syrup	7 oz
5 mL	lemon juice	1 tsp
5 mL	chopped fresh ginger	1 tsp
450 g	wild blueberries	2 cups
250 g	all-purpose flour	9 oz
150 g	granulated sugar	5 ⅓ oz
10 mL	baking powder	2 tsp
100 g	unsalted butter	3 ½ oz
120 mL	35% cream	½ cup

6. Combine the flour, sugar, baking powder, butter and cream in a food processor, and pulse until the dough comes together, no longer than 1 minute.

7. Crumble the dough over the top of the fruit in the ramekins, and bake in a preheated oven at 190°C (375°F) for about 20 minutes, or until the fruit is bubbly and the crust a golden brown. Keep warm.

8. When the granita is set, and before serving, scrape the surface with a fork or spoon to form the granita.

Preparation

1. Chill serving glasses in the freezer.

2. Mix all of the granita ingredients well in a blender and strain.

3. Pour the strained mixture into a shallow tray and place in the freezer until firm (like ice cream).

4. Combine the syrup, lemon juice and ginger in a small saucepan; bring to a boil for 3 minutes.

5. Fill ramekins (or ovenproof dishes) halfway with the blueberries and pour the syrup over top. Set aside.

Assembly

9. Serve the granita in the chilled glasses, atop pretty plates. Garnish with a day lily petal or mint leaf from the garden. Serve the cobbler warm, also on a pretty plate.

Renée's Wild Blueberry Cobbler

Honey Mead Cantaloupe Soup
with Strawberry Ginger Jelly

Sweet and juicy cantaloupes hit the market at the end of summer. And with the new everbearing cultivars being grown in Quebec, strawberries are now available well into fall. This is a very refreshing, easy-to-make cold fruit soup, and it is perfectly accompanied by a glass of chilled mead. Make the strawberry jelly at least 2 hours ahead of time.

4 SERVINGS

INGREDIENTS

JELLY

250 mL	fresh local strawberries	1 cup
45 mL	wildflower honey	3 tbsp
3 mL	chopped fresh ginger	½ tsp
1 leaf (2 g)	gelatin, soaked in cold water, squeezed dry	1 leaf (¼ pkg)

SOUP

1	ripe cantaloupe	1
250 mL	Cuvée du Diable mead (or floral white wine)	1 cup
5 mL	grated fresh ginger	1 tsp
30 mL	wildflower honey	2 tbsp
15 mL	fresh lemon juice	1 tbsp

GARNISH

4	small strawberries	4
1	orange day lily flower (optional)	1
4	lemon balm leaves	4

Preparation

1. To make the strawberry jelly, wash and hull the strawberries and cut them into halves or quarters. Combine with the honey and ginger. Let stand for about 1 hour in a cool place.

2. Place the mixture in a blender container and blend to make a coulis. Strain and discard pulp.

3. Transfer the strained strawberry coulis to a saucepan and bring to a boil; remove from heat and add the softened gelatin. Pour into a small square container sized so that the coulis is 2 cm (¾ in.) deep, and leave in a cool place to set.

4. Remove the rind from the melon and discard. Cut the melon in half, remove the seeds and cut into pieces. Place in the blender. Add the mead, grated ginger, honey and lemon juice. Blend into a smooth purée and set aside in a cool place.

Assembly

5. To serve, cut the jelly into small cubes or other shapes, using a knife. Place the jelly pieces in deep, chilled bowls and cover with the melon soup.

6. Decorate with the 4 remaining strawberries. If your garden is in flower, you can add a few flower petals. Day lilies are delicious and have a lovely texture. Complete the garnish with the lemon balm leaves.

Honey Mead Cantaloupe Soup

ANNE DESJARDINS
COOKS AT
L'EAU À LA BOUCHE
THE SEASONAL CUISINE
OF QUEBEC

PAGE 107

Fall provides a

welcome break from the frenzy of our summer season. The growers and producers are busy harvesting and storing the abundance of colours and flavours the land has to offer.

Fall in the Laurentians means colour, and yellows, ochres, oranges, reds and greens suddenly appear before our eyes as the landscape puts on its brilliant show. In general, September and October weather is cool but pleasant. There's nothing better than rambling through the woods with friends in search of bole-tus and chanterelle mushrooms, or taking a drive to visit a grower, where we can see, smell and touch all the wonderful produce.

At this time of year, the Table de concertation agroalimentaire (an association of agrifood stakeholders in the Laurentians) invites regional chefs to come and discover local producers and their offerings. I like to invite the chefs on my team (and when there's room, the wait staff) to come along, in order to savour the beauty of our region and appreciate its bounty.

Fall

I enjoy taking the road that goes through Mirabel when I travel to visit producers in the Lower Laurentians. In the fall, St.-Joseph-du-Lac abounds with large, well-kept orchards that sag under the weight of ripe fruit. I often drop in on Jude Lavigne to pick apples, pears and his rare mirabelle plums.

Further along the same road, Sylvie D'Amours presides over acres of splendid pumpkins and squash. Turban, Hubbard, pepper and butternut squash abound in myriad shapes and colours.

And Terry Hussey at Insalada is smiling again, as he reaps the rewards of all his painstaking work. All the vegetables he has lovingly tended are finally ready: multicoloured carrots, pink radishes, yellow beets, parsley root, Jerusalem artichokes, kohlrabi, crosnes (Chinese artichokes) and Ratte fingerling potatoes.

Fall truly is the season of plenty in our region, which produces cabbages, cauliflowers, onions, leeks and even finicky artichokes. I return from my outings exhilarated by the rich diversity of nature's wealth. And that's how my recipes take shape. Even if some products are always available and my customers repeatedly ask for them, my recipes evolve along with the seasons to reflect the diversity of our region.

I enjoy cooking with vegetables and find that, in general, people don't know how to prepare them. They are often seen as just a necessary accompaniment to main dishes, and that's a shame. I'm not a vegetarian, but I find that when vegetables are prepared as if they matter and used in recipes that are developed entirely on the basis of their distinctive characteristics, the results are discoveries worth sharing.

Fall also means a plethora of wild mushrooms. It's hard to believe that up until a few years ago no one even thought of collecting them or was even aware that there are many edible mushrooms native to Quebec. Our woods abound with mushrooms of all kinds, with different varieties springing up depending on temperature and rainfall. Of special interest to the chef are the flavourful boletus, the delicate chanterelle (*Cantharellus*), the tasty lobster mushroom (*Hypomyces lactifluorum*) and the puffballs (*Lycoperdum* and *Calvatia*). Their very names inspire me to come up with new recipes.

Our woods and fields are a treasure trove of edible plants. Gérard LeGall is an amateur mushroom collector who knows a great deal about wild edibles, and when he first introduced me to the marinated buds of the ox-eye daisy (*Chrysanthemum leucanthemum*), I found their delicate taste even better than the finest Italian capers I had tried and immediately wanted to use them in a recipe. The first time, I tried something fairly conventional: a medallion of pan-fried monkfish in virgin olive oil served with a fumet of daisy buds and tomato confetti. It was very good, but then I had the idea of combining the tartness of the daisy buds with the fruitiness of apples and the rich, meaty flavour of a pan-seared escalope of fresh duck foie gras. The resulting dish was sublime: the daisy buds were just tart enough to boost the sweetness of the apples and balance the foie gras, perfectly enhancing its succulence. This recipe is now featured on our fall menu every year, even though foie gras is now always in season. For the past few years, our local breeders have been raising very high-quality foie gras ducks year-round that rival their French cousins. Quebeckers with discriminating palates have always liked organ meats and have enthusiastically embraced this new taste.

A PEAR FROM THE VERGER
JUD'POM

FROMAGERIE DU MARCHE

PYRAMIDS OF DELICIOUS GOAT CHEESE

SYLVIE'S BEAUTIFUL GRAPES

AN ABUNDANCE OF SQUASH

THE ENTRANCE
TO THE
RESTAURANT

SYLVIE'S PRIDE AND JOY

THE GREENHOUSES OF MIRABEL

FERME-NEUVE'S
MARVELLOUS MEAD

Crisp, Crunchy Fall Salad
of Julienned Hubbard Squash, Empire Apples, Pomegranate Seeds, Cucumber, with Cider Vinaigrette

 Here's a quintessential fall recipe. As with all salads, the key is to use top-quality ingredients. Greenhouses in the Laurentians supply delectable greens throughout the fall and even winter, and local orchards provide apples that can be used to put together delicious salads.

4 SERVINGS

INGREDIENTS

100 mL	organic canola oil	⅜ cup
30 mL	natural cider vinegar	2 tbsp
	salt, to taste	
	Tabasco sauce	
200 g	Hubbard squash, peeled and finely julienned	7 oz
	vegetable oil	
50 g	pomegranate seeds	1 ¾ oz
100 g	unpeeled Empire apples, cored and finely julienned	3 ½ oz
100 g	cucumber, julienned	3 ½ oz
2	large basil leaves, chopped	2
2	green onions, finely chopped	2
200 g	greens of your choice	7 oz
4	Goat's Milk Cheddar Tuiles (see page 19)	4

Preparation

1. Make a vinaigrette with the canola oil and cider vinegar. Season to taste with salt and Tabasco and set aside.

2. In a skillet, sauté 100 g (3 ½ oz) of the julienned squash in vegetable oil. Salt and set aside.

3. Combine the remaining julienned squash, 25 g (¾ oz) of the pomegranate seeds, apple, cucumber, basil and half the green onions.

4. Add the vinaigrette and stir well.

Assembly

5. Arrange the greens on chilled plates, and place the vegetable mixture in the centre. Garnish with the fried squash and sprinkle with pomegranate seeds.

6. Sprinkle with the remaining green onions. Decorate with Goat's Milk Cheddar Tuiles.

Crisp, Crunchy Fall Salad

Atlantic Salmon Tartare
with Two Mustards, Wild Ginger and Salicornia

At this time of year, I get a weekly visit from François Brouillard. He wanders the fields and forests, lakeshores and riverbanks, collecting wild herbs, vegetables and mushrooms that are little known or have been long forgotten. Salicornia, or sea asparagus, grows in the salt marshes of the St. Lawrence River and is a perfect complement to fish and seafood. Wild ginger (Asarum canadense) grows in the woods throughout Quebec. Its roots are smaller than its oriental counterpart, and it is very aromatic, with a more complex flavour.

4 SERVINGS

INGREDIENTS

	salt, to taste	
	Tabasco sauce	
45 mL	lemon juice	3 tbsp
10 mL	freshly grated wild ginger (or regular ginger root)	2 tsp
5 mL	Dijon mustard	1 tsp
10 mL	grainy mustard	2 tsp
90 mL	extra-virgin olive oil	6 tbsp
2	green onions, finely chopped	2
240 g	extra-fresh Atlantic salmon fillet, finely diced	8 ½ oz
10 mL	trout caviar	2 tsp
200 g	salicornia, blanched, and trimmed of tough stems if necessary	7 oz

Preparation

1. Combine salt, Tabasco, lemon juice, wild ginger, the two mustards and extra-virgin olive oil to create a vinaigrette.

Assembly

2. Combine three-quarters of the vinaigrette, the green onions and the diced salmon. Shape the tartare into mounds on well-chilled plates. Top with the trout caviar.

3. Mix a little vinaigrette with the salicornia. Arrange the salicornia around the salmon tartare and drizzle with the remaining vinaigrette.

Atlantic Salmon Tartare with Two Mustards

**ANNE DESJARDINS
COOKS AT
L'EAU À LA BOUCHE**
THE SEASONAL CUISINE
OF QUEBEC

PAGE 117

Jerusalem Artichoke Soup

with Miniature Escalope of Fresh Duck Foie Gras and Truffled Croutons

 Here's a sophisticated soup for a festive dinner. Make it several hours ahead of time then serve it in a large tureen (or in a teapot, like I do at the restaurant). Pour the soup directly into each bowl over the escalope and the brioche.

4 SERVINGS

INGREDIENTS

200 g	Jerusalem artichokes	7 oz
1	large onion	1
5 mL	butter	1 tsp
100 mL	white wine	⅜ cup
500 mL	chicken stock (see page 18)	2 cups
20 cubes	brioche (cut in 2 cm [¾ in.] cubes)	20 cubes
50 mL	extra-virgin olive oil	3 tbsp
20 mL	white truffle oil	3 tbsp
4	fresh duck foie gras escalopes, 50 g (1 ¾ oz) each	4
	salt, to taste	
30 g	fresh truffle, thinly sliced (optional)	1 oz
	fresh chives, finely chopped	
	or	
1	green onion, finely minced	1

Preparation

1. *Peel the Jerusalem artichokes and onion and cut into pieces. In a saucepan, melt the butter and sweat the onions. Add the Jerusalem artichoke pieces (reserving 1 large piece), then add the white wine and chicken stock. Simmer over low heat for 30 minutes. Put the mixture in a blender and blend. Season to taste and set aside.*

2. *To make croutons, preheat the oven to 205°C (400°F). Place the bread cubes in a bowl; add the olive oil and salt, and stir well. Spread on a baking sheet and toast in the oven for 8 minutes until golden brown. Sprinkle with the truffle oil. Remove and set the croutons aside.*

Assembly

3. *To serve, peel and julienne the reserved piece of Jerusalem artichoke.*

4. *In a preheated heavy or nonstick skillet, sear the foie gras over medium heat until brown on both sides and soft to the touch. Season with salt and drain on paper towels.*

5. *Place 5 croutons and an escalope of foie gras in each warmed soup bowl. Add a little julienned Jerusalem artichoke, a few drops of truffle oil, truffle slices (if using) and chives.*

6. *Ladle or pour the soup into the bowls and serve.*

ANNE DESJARDINS
COOKS AT
L'EAU À LA BOUCHE
THE SEASONAL CUISINE
OF QUEBEC

PAGE 120

*Jerusalem
Artichoke Soup*

Braised Sweetbreads
Crosnes and Multi-coloured Carrots Flavoured with Star Anise

 This sweet and sour dish is lightly spiced with star anise, a surprising yet subtle ingredient. Sometimes as an accompaniment I add braised or sautéed fennel, another anise flavour that works well in this recipe.

4 SERVINGS

INGREDIENTS

400 g	heart sweetbreads (see page 20)	14 oz
50 mL	Pernod	3 tbsp
8	star anise pods	8
4	small red carrots	4
4	small yellow carrots	4
4	small orange carrots	4
50 g	butter	1 ¾ oz
	lemon juice	
20	crosnes (Chinese artichokes)	20
	or	
½	fennel bulb, thinly sliced	½
	chopped chives	
	salt, to taste	

Preparation

1. Cook the sweetbreads, adding the Pernod and 3 star anise pods to the basic recipe. Reserve the braising liquid.

2. Peel the carrots and blanch. Set aside.

Assembly

3. In a small skillet, gently sauté the sweetbreads in a little butter. Add the reserved cooking liquid from the sweetbreads and 1 star anise pod. Simmer over low heat for a few minutes to reheat the sweetbreads. Correct the seasoning with a few drops of lemon juice. Add a little butter to finish.

4. In a little butter, sauté the crosnes and the carrots. Add chives and salt to taste.

5. Serve on heated plates, garnished with star anise pods.

Braised Sweetbreads

ANNE DESJARDINS COOKS AT L'EAU À LA BOUCHE
THE SEASONAL CUISINE OF QUEBEC

Fresh Pan-seared Duck Foie Gras

with Apple, Grape and Daisy Bud Medley and Sweet and Sour Apple Must Sauce

 My customers adore warm foie gras, and rightly so. Its mild flavour makes it very versatile. And it's easier to make than it looks. If you choose to prepare the apple chip garnish, give yourself plenty of time to make this dish.

4 SERVINGS

INGREDIENTS

1	apple (optional)	*1*
2	shallots, minced	*2*
2	apples, peeled, cored and finely diced (reserve peels)	*2*
75 mL	natural cider vinegar	*5 tbsp*
200 mL	apple must	*¾ cup*
400 mL	reduced duck stock or poultry stock (see page 18)	*1 ⅝ cups*
4	long peppercorns	*4*
20	seedless red grapes, halved	*20*
100 mL	daisy buds (or capers)	*⅜ cup*
45 mL	butter	*3 tbsp*
	fresh rosemary sprigs	
	salt, to taste	
4	fresh duck foie gras escalopes, 100 g (3 ½ oz) each	*4*

Preparation

1. To prepare the optional apple chip garnish, slice the apple paper thin using a mandoline. Sprinkle lightly with ground long pepper if you like. Bake in a 135°C (200°F) oven for 1 ½ hours or leave overnight in the cold oven with the pilot light on.

2. In a small saucepan, cook the shallots with the apple peels until golden brown, over medium heat. Deglaze with the cider vinegar. Add the apple must and reduce until nearly dry. Add the stock and reduce again. When there is 300 mL (1 ¼ cups) of liquid left, strain the sauce. Season to taste, add the long peppercorns and set aside.

3. In a skillet, quickly cook the diced apple, grapes and daisy buds in a little butter. Add a little chopped rosemary. Do not overcook. You want the fruit to retain its shape and have some texture. Season with salt to taste and keep warm.

Assembly

4. In a nonstick skillet, sear the foie gras escalopes, a few minutes per side, over medium-high heat to a melting texture. Season with salt to taste and remove from heat. Drain on paper towels and keep warm.

5. Arrange the apple medley on heated plates and place the escalopes on top. Top with sauce. Garnish with dried apple chips and rosemary sprigs.

ANNE DESJARDINS
COOKS AT
L'EAU À LA BOUCHE
THE SEASONAL CUISINE
OF QUEBEC

PAGE 126

Fresh Pan-seared Duck Foie Gras

Three Vegetables Au Gratin for Fall

Sautéed Barley with Butternut Squash, Sun-dried Tomatoes and Aged Cheddar

Spaghetti Squash with Mushrooms, Toasted Pine Nuts and Wabassee Cheese

Pumpkin Soup with Fresh Goat Cheese Croutons

At the restaurant, I serve these as a trio of small vegetarian dishes. At home, you can put them in serving dishes in the centre of the table so that people can help themselves. You can also serve the elements individually as first courses or side dishes.

Sylvie D'Amours in St.-Joseph-du-Lac specializes in growing different varieties of pumpkins. The Cucurbitaceae family includes many familiar vegetables, including cucumbers and melons. Squashes and pumpkins are native to North America and were a staple in the diet of First Nations peoples. And yet, pumpkin is not often used today, apart from the large, least flavourful varieties used at Hallowe'en. Pumpkin is actually delicious and can be used in many different dishes besides pumpkin pie.

Sautéed Barley
with Butternut Squash, Sun-dried Tomatoes and Aged Cheddar

Ingredients

1 bunch	fresh basil leaves	1 bunch
125 mL	sun-dried tomatoes	½ cup
250 mL	pearl barley	1 cup
450 mL	chicken stock (see page 18)	1 ¾ cups
100 g	mushrooms (wild or cultivated), cut into pieces	3 ½ oz
100 g	butternut squash, peeled and diced	3 ½ oz
30 mL	virgin olive oil	2 tbsp
2	green onions, sliced	2
5 mL	grated fresh ginger	1 tsp
	salt, to taste	
100 g	aged cheddar, grated	3 ½ oz

Preparation

1. Grease 4 small ovenproof ramekins. Chop the basil, reserving 4 leaves for garnish. Soak the sun-dried tomatoes in cold water for 15 minutes to rehydrate and chop thinly. Cook the barley in the chicken stock in a saucepan for about 20 minutes over medium heat and set aside.

2. In a skillet, sauté the mushrooms and diced squash in a little olive oil. Add the green onion, basil and ginger. Set aside.

3. In another skillet, sauté the cooked barley in a little olive oil, over medium heat, adding the tomatoes, mushrooms and diced squash. Season with salt to taste. Add half the cheese and fill the ramekins with the barley mixture. Top with the remaining cheese and set aside.

Assembly

4. Preheat the oven to 205°C (400°F). Put the ramekins in the oven and bake for 12 to 15 minutes, depending on their size, until bubbly hot and golden.

Spaghetti Squash
with Mushrooms, Toasted Pine Nuts and Wabassee Cheese

Wabassee is a mild, surface-ripened cheese from Fromagerie Le P'tit Train du Nord in Mont-Laurier.

INGREDIENTS

1	small spaghetti squash	1
120 g	wild mushrooms (*boletus* or *chanterelles*) or *cultivated mushrooms* (*shiitake* or *oyster*)	4 ¼ oz
50 mL	virgin olive oil	3 tbsp
50 g	toasted pine nuts	1 ¾ oz
2	green onions, minced	2
	chopped fresh parsley	
120 g	Wabassee cheese, grated	4 ¼ oz
	salt, to taste	
	Tabasco sauce	

PREPARATION

1. Halve and seed the spaghetti squash. Bake in the oven, on a greased baking sheet, cut-side down for 30 minutes at 175°C (350°F), or halved, seeded and covered with plastic wrap in the microwave for 9 minutes on high. Using a fork, separate the spaghetti-like fibres of the squash. Set aside.

2. Sauté the mushrooms in the olive oil and add the squash, pine nuts, green onion, parsley and half the cheese. Season with salt and Tabasco to taste. Fill small greased au gratin dishes with the mixture, top with the remaining cheese and set aside.

ASSEMBLY

3. Preheat the oven to 205°C (400°F) and bake for 15 minutes. Serve immediately.

Pumpkin Soup
with Fresh Goat Cheese Croutons

The soup and croutons can be prepared several hours in advance.

INGREDIENTS

1	medium pumpkin	1
15 mL	butter	1 tbsp
1	large onion, sliced	1
100 mL	white wine	⅜ cup
500 mL	chicken stock (see page 18)	2 cups
	salt, to taste	
4 thin slices	sourdough or country bread	4 thin slices
50 mL	extra-virgin olive oil	3 tbsp
50 mL	pumpkin seed oil	3 tbsp
100 g	fresh goat cheese, cut into 4 slices (25 g [1 oz] each)	3 ½ oz
8	fresh chives, finely chopped	8

PREPARATION

1. Bake the pumpkins in the oven at 200°C (400°F) for about 25 minutes if miniature, or at 175°C (350°F) for up to an hour if large. When done, cut off the top third of the pumpkins and scoop out the flesh, taking care to keep the rind intact. Remove the seeds and set aside the flesh.

2. In a saucepan, melt the butter and sauté the onion until golden brown. Add the pumpkin flesh, white wine and chicken stock. Simmer for 20 minutes. Blend the mixture in a blender. Salt to taste and set aside.

3. Preheat the oven to 205°C (400°F). Place the bread slices in a bowl and sprinkle with olive oil and half the pumpkin seed oil, coating well. Transfer the croutons to a baking sheet and bake for 6 minutes until toasted. Remove from oven and set aside.

ASSEMBLY

4. Preheat the broiler.

5. Place the cheese on the toasted bread slices and broil for 2 minutes.

6. Ladle the soup into shallow bowls. Top each with a goat cheese crouton, a few drops of pumpkin seed oil and chopped chives.

"Napoleon"
of Flash-seared Atlantic Salmon Escalopes, Spinach and Butternut Squash with Creamy Olive Oil Emulsion

 Here's an easy, light-tasting recipe that makes use of seasonal ingredients.

4 SERVINGS

INGREDIENTS

120 mL	warm creamy olive oil emulsion (see page 21)	½ cup
2	green onions, minced	2
	juice and zest of 1 lemon	
45 mL	extra-virgin olive oil	3 tbsp
600 g	fresh baby spinach leaves, washed	1 ⅓ lb
300 g	butternut squash, peeled and julienned	10 ½ oz
12	small, thin slices of fresh Atlantic salmon, cut from the same piece (50 g [1 ¾ oz] each), skinned	12
	salt, to taste	

Preparation

1. To the olive oil emulsion, add half the green onion, half the lemon zest and the lemon juice. Set aside.

Assembly

2. To serve, heat 3 heavy or nonstick skillets and put a little olive oil in each one. Stir-fry the spinach in the first skillet, sauté the julienned squash in the second and quickly sauté the salmon over high heat in the last one, less than 30 seconds per side, so that the pieces are cooked but still intact. Season each skillet with salt to taste and sprinkle the salmon with the remaining green onion and zest.

3. Heat the olive oil emulsion.

4. On heated plates, alternate slices of salmon, julienned squash and spinach to form a stack, ending with a slice of salmon. Top with the olive oil emulsion.

**ANNE DESJARDINS
COOKS AT
L'EAU À LA BOUCHE**
THE SEASONAL CUISINE
OF QUEBEC

PAGE 134

"Napoleon"

Skate, Chanterelles, Princess Scallops
Grilled Pepper Squash and Onions, with Lime-flavoured Shellfish Sauce

Fish is so quick and easy that it makes cooking a breeze, but it's important to find a reliable fish purveyor. Also, fish must never be overcooked. As soon as it has turned opaque, it's ready to eat. At the restaurant, I like to cook skate on the bone.

Princess scallops are young sea scallops in the shell that we get from the Magdalen Islands in Quebec from spring to fall.

4 SERVINGS

INGREDIENTS

½	pepper squash, peeled and thickly sliced	½
	salt, to taste	
30 mL	extra-virgin olive oil	2 tbsp
2	large onions, diced	2
4	fresh skate fillets, 160 g (5 ⅔ oz) each, cleaned	4
200 g	fresh chanterelles	7 oz
8	Princess scallops, shelled, muscle removed	
200 mL	stock made from shellfish shells (see page 19)	¾ cup
15 mL	butter	1 tbsp
	juice of 1 lime	
	Tabasco sauce	

Preparation

1. Grill the squash slices under the broiler for 6 to 8 minutes, until tender and golden brown. Season with salt and set aside.

2. In a skillet, sauté the onions in a little olive oil until golden brown and soft. Season and keep warm.

Assembly

3. In a heavy or nonstick skillet, pan-fry the skate fillets in a little olive oil a few minutes per side, over medium heat. Remove from the skillet and keep warm.

4. Quickly sauté the chanterelles and the scallops in a little olive oil in the same skillet. Remove and set aside.

5. Deglaze the skillet with the stock. Simmer to reduce by half, add a little butter and correct the seasoning with salt, lime juice and Tabasco.

6. Serve on heated plates. Place the skate on top of the grilled squash, surrounded by scallops, chanterelles and onions. Top with the sauce.

Skate, Chanterelles, Princess Scallops

Lamb Prepared Two Ways

Roasted Loin in an Almond Sage Crust and Braised Shoulder in a Potato "Napoleon," with Shiitake Mushrooms and Root Vegetables

This recipe features different cuts of lamb and fall vegetables, and makes for a festive meal. This recipe is made in stages: the shoulder is braised, the loin is cooked just before serving and the vegetables are prepared separately.

8 SERVINGS

INGREDIENTS

1	small lamb shoulder, bone in	1
5	whole shallots	5
3	garlic cloves, peeled	3
500 mL	red wine	2 cups
20	fresh sage leaves	20
	salt, to taste	
1	large carrot	1
1	large parsnip	1
1	small celery root	1
1	parsley root	1
200 g	ground almonds	7 oz
2	Yukon Gold potatoes	2
150 g	clarified unsalted butter	5 ⅓ oz
500 g	lamb loin	1 ⅛ lb
	extra-virgin olive oil	
45 mL	Dijon mustard	3 tbsp
400 g	fresh shiitake mushrooms	14 oz

Preparation

1. Place the lamb shoulder in an enamelled cast-iron pot (if available) with the shallots, garlic and red wine. Add 5 sage leaves and season generously with salt. Cover and braise in a very low-temperature oven (120°C [250°F]) for 4 ½ hours.

2. Peel the root vegetables. Cut them into 1 × 1 cm (½ in. × ½ in.) sticks and cut diagonally at 1 cm (½ in.) intervals. Blanch the root vegetables and set aside.

3. Toast the ground almonds on a baking sheet in a 175°C (350°F) oven for 8 minutes until golden. Chop 7 of the sage leaves.

4. When the lamb shoulder is done, remove it from the pot, debone and keep the meat warm. Strain the cooking juices into a small saucepan. Simmer to reduce by half and correct the seasoning. Set aside.

5. Cut the potatoes into thin slices and poach in the clarified butter over medium-low heat until tender.

6. Prepare the napoleons as follows: Top 1 slice of cooked potato with 15 mL (1 tbsp) boned shoulder meat. Repeat the operation twice, to end up with three layers. Prepare 8 napoleons and keep warm. Be careful: they tend to tip over!

Assembly

7. In a skillet, sear the lamb loin in a little olive oil, over high heat. Season with salt, remove from the skillet and baste with the Dijon mustard. Add chopped sage leaves, and cover with the roasted ground almonds. Bake in the oven at 205°C (400°F) for 5 minutes and set aside to rest in a warm place.

8. In the meantime, sauté the shütakes in a little olive oil in a skillet over high heat. Add the root vegetables, reheat and season.

9. Cut the lamb loin into eight 60 g (2 oz) servings. Serve on large heated plates, with the medallion of loin atop the potato napoleon. Surround with the shitake–root vegetable mixture. Garnish with the remaining sage leaves.

Lamb Prepared Two Ways

Roast Beef Striploin
with Ceylon Tea Sauce, and Puréed and Fried Celery Root

It's hard to imagine a more typical fall meal than roast beef with a tasty root vegetable purée. Celery root makes it original and delicious. The sauce is made with strong black tea, which my grandmother used for deglazing the pan.

4 SERVINGS

INGREDIENTS

1	large starchy potato, peeled and quartered	1
3	large celery roots, peeled and cut into large pieces	3
6	large garlic cloves, peeled	6
200 g	butter, softened	7 oz
	vegetable oil	
	salt, to taste	
15 mL	Dijon mustard	1 tbsp
700 g	beef tenderloin, trimmed	1 ½ lb
1	onion, sliced	1
500 mL	Ceylon tea, prepared very strong	2 cups

Preparation

1. *Boil the potato, 2 celery roots and 3 garlic cloves. When tender, drain off the water, steam dry, and purée (mash and sieve, or pass through a food mill or ricer), adding 125 g (4 ½ oz) softened butter. Keep warm.*

2. *Thinly slice a quarter of the remaining celery root. Add a little vegetable oil to a frying pan, and fry until crispy. Season with salt and drain on paper towels.*

3. *Cut the remaining celery root into large sticks. Baste with 20 g (1 to 2 tbsp) of butter, season with salt and place on a baking sheet.*

4. *Preheat the oven to 220ºC (425ºF). Spread the mustard on the beef and salt generously. Place 3 garlic cloves, the sliced onion and the beef in a drip pan.*

Assembly

5. *Place the celery root sticks and the beef in the oven to sear for 5 minutes at 220ºC (425ºF). Remove the celery root sticks from the oven and set aside. Lower the heat to 160ºC (325ºF) and continue roasting the beef. For medium-rare beef, allow approximately 15 minutes. A meat thermometer will give you more accurate results (50ºC [130ºF] for medium rare).*

6. *Remove from the oven and let rest for at least 10 minutes in a warm place.*

7. *To make the sauce, place the drip pan over high heat and deglaze the juices with the tea. Simmer until reduced by half. Strain the liquid into a small saucepan and discard the onions and garlic. Season to taste and add the remaining butter.*

8. *Carve the tenderloin and place the striploin slices on heated plates, with the purée, baked celery root sticks and fried celery root slices.*

Roast Beef Striploin

ANNE DESJARDINS COOKS AT L'EAU À LA BOUCHE
THE SEASONAL CUISINE OF QUEBEC

Loin of Venison
Red Wine Sauce with Peppercorns and Juniper Berries, and Jerusalem Artichoke Purée

 The key to this dish is using the best venison you can find. I prefer to get mine from the magnificent Harp Farm in Boileau, in the Outaouais region of Quebec, which produces venison of exceptionally fine quality.

6 SERVINGS

INGREDIENTS

8	large Jerusalem artichokes	8
150 g	butter, softened	5 ⅓ oz
	salt, to taste	
1.2 kg	loin of venison, cut into six 200 g (7 oz) steaks	2 ⅔ lb
15 mL	sunflower oil	1 tbsp
1	shallot, minced	1
50 mL	balsamic vinegar (aged minimum 10 years)	3 tbsp
200 mL	dry red wine	¾ cup
6	juniper berries	6
60 mL	pink and green peppercorns	4 tbsp
200 mL	venison stock or veal stock (see page 18)	¾ cup

Preparation

1. Peel the Jerusalem artichokes, cut them into large pieces and boil until the pieces are soft enough to purée. Drain well, return to hot pan and allow to steam dry for a few minutes (this is very important or else the purée will be too watery). Purée and add 100 g (3 ½ oz) softened butter. Season with salt to taste and set aside.

Assembly

2. Salt the slices of venison loin. In a heavy skillet, heat a little sunflower oil and a little butter, and sear the venison over high heat just as you would a steak (a few minutes per side only; to desired degree of doneness). Remove from skillet and keep warm. Add the minced shallot to the same skillet and deglaze with the balsamic vinegar and red wine. Add the juniper berries, peppercorns and the venison or veal stock, and simmer to reduce by half. Add 50 g (1 ¾ oz) butter and season with salt to taste.

3. Place the purée and venison on heated plates and top with the sauce.

Loin of Venison

Riopelle de l'Isle Cheese
Served with Plums Macerated in Spiced Port and Toasted Almonds

 Riopelle de l'Isle is a soft raw-milk, triple-cream cheese with a white rind that comes from l'Île aux Grues, near Montmagny. I like to serve it in late summer or in the fall with plums from Jude Lavigne's orchard. He tends his orchard with care and picks his plums only when they are ripened to perfection. Take the cheese out of the fridge at least 2 hours before serving.

4 SERVINGS

INGREDIENTS

100 g	slivered almonds	3 ½ oz
16	blue prune plums	16
500 mL	red port	2 cups
15 mL	balsamic vinegar	1 tbsp
1	star anise pod	1
1	long peppercorn	1
400 g	Riopelle de l'Isle cheese	14 oz
	sourdough bread	

Preparation

1. Dry-roast the almonds on a baking sheet at 205°C (400°F) for 8 to 10 minutes. Pit the plums and cut into quarters. Bring the port to a boil in a small saucepan, then add the vinegar and spices. Simmer until reduced by half.

2. Pour the liquid over the plums, add the almonds and macerate for at least a few hours. Remove the whole spices.

Assembly

3. Serve a piece of cheese with plums to each guest, along with some slices of sourdough bread.

Riopelle de l'Isle Cheese

ANNE DESJARDINS COOKS AT L'EAU À LA BOUCHE
THE SEASONAL CUISINE OF QUEBEC

Hazelnut Cake

with Whipped Cream, Caramelized Apples, Hazelnuts and Maple Syrup, Flavoured with Star Anise

This recipe uses very little flour. It's not overly sweet and it's very easy to make. Try it with one of the more than 30 varieties of apples from Jude Lavigne's orchard, Jud'Pom, in Oka.

8 SERVINGS

INGREDIENTS

5	egg yolks	5
120 g	granulated sugar	4 oz
250 mL	ground hazelnuts	1 cup
22.5 mL	all-purpose flour	1 ½ tbsp
15 mL	baking powder	1 tbsp
5	egg whites	5
4	cooking apples (Empire or Cortland)	4
5 mL	lemon juice	1 tsp
150 mL	35% cream	⅝ cup
15 mL	maple sugar (or white sugar)	1 tbsp
5 mL	ground star anise	1 tsp
60 g	butter	2 oz
45 mL	chopped hazelnuts	3 tbsp
75 mL	maple syrup	5 tbsp
	whipped cream	

Preparation

1. Preheat the oven to 205°C (400°F).

2. Beat the egg yolks and half the granulated sugar until light and creamy. Gently stir in the ground hazelnuts, flour and baking powder. Beat the egg whites with the remaining granulated sugar and gently fold into the egg yolk mixture.

3. Immediately spread the mixture in a 22.5 × 27.5 × 6.25 cm (9 × 11 × 2 in.) cake pan, cover with parchment and bake for 15 to 20 minutes, or until a knife inserted in the cake comes out clean. Cool slightly, then unmould onto a cooling rack. Set aside.

4. Peel, seed and thinly slice the apples. Place in a bowl of cold water with a little lemon juice.

5. Whip the cream with the maple sugar and star anise until the cream forms stiff peaks. Refrigerate.

Assembly

6. To serve, melt half the butter in a heavy skillet and caramelize the apples and chopped hazelnuts. Add the maple syrup and a pinch of ground star anise. Reduce until syrupy, then remove from heat and add the rest of the butter to thicken.

7. Serve pieces of the cake on dessert plates, and surround each piece with caramelized apples and syrup. Top each serving of cake with a dollop of whipped cream.

Hazelnut Cake with Whipped Cream

I love fall (...)

The growers and producers are busy harvesting and storing the abundance of colours and flavours the land has to offer...

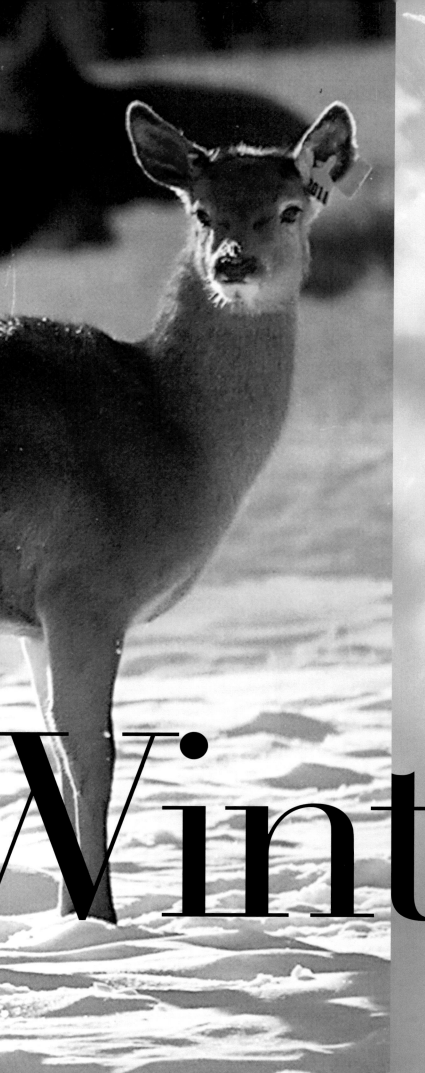

Winter

Although a white blanket of snow covers the world, it's warm and cozy indoors and the harvests we have put by and the skills of our local producers continue to nourish us throughout this long season. The food we serve in winter is every bit as inventive and appetizing as at other times of the year.

In the winter, northern cooks have to draw on their creativity. Fortunately, with advances in technology, greens, herbs and vegetables can be grown at a relatively reasonable cost in greenhouses. We have also adopted the methods of our European ancestors and First Nations peoples for curing and smoking fish.

Farmed trout, Arctic char, the delectable white caviar of the whitefish, red trout caviar and black sturgeon caviar — all available from the lakes of the Abitibi-Témiscaming region — add variety to the winter menu.

Since our local growers have started growing and storing celery root, yellow beets and Hubbard squash, we can enjoy them even in the dead of winter. At that time, we also turn to such hearty but under-appreciated grains and legumes as wild rice, barley and buckwheat, along with pumpkinseed oil and mead vinegar. Exotic varieties of poultry, foie gras, meat and venison are still available, so I can prepare dishes using exclusively regional products even in February.

Moreover, excellent new Quebec cheeses have flooded the market in recent years; there are now probably more than a hundred varieties in all. Although not all have been successful, some — especially those made with raw milk (or heat-treated milk, to be more accurate) — are revelations of incredible flavour. As far back as I can remember, basic cheeses have had a place at our family table. But after travelling to Europe, where cheese is an integral part of the meal and some cheeses are protected by an "appellation d'origine controllée" (a label guaranteeing its origin), I discovered the pleasures of cooking and ending a meal with cheese.

Now, we have an almost bewildering array of cheeses to choose from. In the winter, I enjoy making fondue for my family using Vacherin des Bois-Francs, or a raclette of Wabassee from Mont-Laurier accompanied by Ratte fingerling potatoes. My winter discovery menu features a walnut tart with Victor et Berthold cheese from Martin Guilbault's Fromagerie du Champ à la Meule in Lanaudière and ravioli stuffed with goat cheese from Bergerie du Troupeau Bénit in Chatham, near Lachute.

Yannick Achin, from the cheese shop at the St.-Jérôme market, is an invaluable source of advice and information about all the new cheeses. Many of our producers have made remarkable progress, learning quickly, adjusting their recipes and applying newly acquired techniques. I believe we should applaud their achievements and encourage excellence, as their vitality is important to the survival of our local agriculture in the context of global competition.

Finally, I'd like to say that in spite of — or thanks to — our location north of the forty-seventh parallel, we have a rich, full bounty of ingredients at our disposal. The unique flavours of the Laurentian countryside, along with our dedicated artisans, farmers and producers, provide a soulful, satisfying milieu in which to cook.

CLAUDE DESROCHERS IN HIS MEADERY IN FERME-NEUVE

Maple-Marinated Trout and Fennel,

Mirabel Greens and Pine Nuts, with Fennel Juice and Olive Oil Vinaigrette

The ingredients used here are easy to find even in winter, and the subtle flavours complement the trout nicely. The fish is "cooked" by marinating it for several hours.

4 SERVINGS

INGREDIENTS

50 g	coarse salt	1 ¾ oz
100 mL	maple syrup	⅜ cup
5 mL	black peppercorns	1 tsp
1	star anise pod, coarsely ground	1
	juice and zest of 1 lemon	
15 mL	Pernod	1 tbsp
250 g	fresh trout fillet (or salmon or Arctic char)	9 oz
1	fennel bulb (with leaves if possible)	1
125 mL	flavourful extra-virgin olive oil	½ cup
2	green onions, minced	2
	salt, to taste	
100 g	mini salad greens	3 ½ oz
30 mL	freshly toasted pine nuts	2 tbsp

Preparation

1. *Prepare the marinade by combining the coarse salt, maple syrup, peppercorns and star anise. Add 15 mL (1 tbsp) lemon juice and the Pernod.*

2. *Place the trout fillet in a shallow dish, cover with the maple marinade and marinate in the refrigerator for 3 hours. Remove the fillet from the marinade. Pat dry, cover with plastic wrap, and refrigerate.*

3. *Cut the fennel bulb in half and juice half of it in a juicer to obtain about 125 mL (½ cup) of juice. Set aside. Using a mandoline, slice the other half of the fennel bulb into paper-thin sheets. Chop the fennel leaves to yield about 30 mL (2 tbsp). Save a few leaves for garnish.*

Assembly

4. *Make a vinaigrette by combining the olive oil, fennel juice, 15 mL (1 tbsp) lemon juice, green onion and chopped fennel leaves. Add salt and pepper to taste. Pour the vinaigrette over the sliced fennel and the greens. Mix well and add the toasted pine nuts.*

5. *Cut the marinated trout fillet into thin slices. On chilled plates, arrange the fennel and greens in a 7.5-cm (3-in.) circle. Fan out the trout pieces. Pour the reserved juices over the fennel and salad greens. Garnish with fennel leaves and lemon zest.*

Maple-Marinated Trout and Fennel

Medallions of Fresh Duck Foie Gras
"En Torchon" with Six Spices, Mead Jelly and Spiced Brioche

Here's a recipe that I've been making at L'Eau à la Bouche for a few years. I used to cook my fresh duck foie gras in the oven in a terrine set in a pan of water, but the results were unreliable. My friend Denise Cornelier, a Montreal-area caterer, taught me this modern method of "poaching" foie gras. I've adapted it with my own choice of ingredients.

When I discovered Claude Desrochers' wonderful mead, Cuvée du Diable, which he makes at his farm in Ferme-Neuve, I was inspired to combine it with the foie gras and spices that give this recipe its distinctive character.

At the restaurant, we serve this dish with a spiced brioche and salad greens. What makes this recipe easy is that the foie gras can be prepared up to a week in advance. It is actually better if it has at least a day for the flavours to meld. Make the mead jelly on the day you plan to serve it and pick up a fresh brioche from your favourite bakery.

Serve as an elegant first course or with aperitifs. Try it with a glass of Cuvée du Diable mead!

6 SERVINGS

INGREDIENTS

1	lobe of raw, fresh mulard duck foie gras, about 500 g (1 ⅛ lb)	1
375 mL	Cuvée du Diable mead (or sweet, floral, oak-aged white wine)	1 ½ cups
15 mL	finely ground spices, mixed (a few pinches each of ground star anise, allspice, cardamom, pink pepper, black pepper and juniper berries)	1 tbsp
6 g	salt	¼ oz
3 leaves (6 g)	gelatin, soaked in cold water, squeezed dry	3 leaves (¾ pkg)
	brioche or toast	

Preparation

1. Allow the foie gras to approach room temperature for 10 minutes or so, and carefully separate the lobes. Remove the network of veins with tweezers or a paring knife.

2. Place the foie gras pieces in a deep dish and sprinkle with 45 mL (3 tbsp) mead. Add the spices and salt, evenly distributing the seasoning. Cover with plastic wrap and refrigerate for 24 hours.

3. The next day, spread out a 30- × 60-cm (12- × 24-in.) sheet of plastic wrap. Place half of the foie gras on the plastic wrap and form a "log" about 3.8 cm (1 ½ in.) in diameter by rolling the foie gras pieces in the plastic wrap. Do the same with the remaining foie gras. Chill the 2 logs for at least 2 hours in the refrigerator.

4. Tightly wrap the logs in plastic wrap, securing the ends with string. Immerse the wrapped foie gras in barely simmering water and cook for 3 minutes. The plastic wrap will not melt and will seal the foie gras.

5. Drain and refrigerate for at least a day.

6. In a small saucepan, heat the mead to the boiling point and boil for 1 minute to evaporate the alcohol. Remove from heat. Dissolve the softened gelatin in the hot mead. Pour into a dish with sides, or a 10- × 15-cm (4- × 6-in.) loaf pan and allow to set. Once cool, refrigerate until ready to use.

7. Cut the mead jelly into small cubes.

Assembly

8. Remove the plastic wrap from the fois gras logs and with a thin-bladed, hot knife, cut each one into 9 slices (3 slices per serving).

9. Serve on chilled plates with cubes of mead jelly and slices of brioche or toast.

Medallions of Fresh Duck Foie Gras

Venison Tartare

Julienned Yellow Beets and Yellow Beet Jelly with Purslane, Chard and Shavings of Sheep's Milk Cheese

 Venison from Boileau is an exceptional delicacy, lean and very healthy. It is perfect for making tartare, a word first used in Belgium to mean raw meat combined with seasonings. Here's my version of it.

This dish also makes an unusual and delicious appetizer.

4 SERVINGS

INGREDIENTS

3	large yellow beets	3
30 mL	natural cider vinegar	2 tbsp
	salt, to taste	
1 ½ leaves (3 g)	gelatin, soaked in cold water, squeezed dry	1 ½ leaves (¼ pkg)
250 g	lean red deer meat	9 oz
60 mL	organic canola oil	¼ cup
5 mL	Dijon mustard	1 tsp
5 mL	maple syrup	1 tsp
3	green onions, minced	3
50 g	sheep's milk cheese shavings	1 ¾ oz
100 g	baby purslane and Swiss chard (or endives and radicchio)	2 cups

Preparation

1. *Boil 2 beets with their skin on until cooked. In the meantime, juice the other beet in a juicer to obtain 125 mL (½ cup) of juice. Pour the juice into a small saucepan with 5 mL (1 tsp) cider vinegar. Bring to a boil and season with salt to taste. Add the softened gelatin to the hot juice. Pour into a small shallow dish and place in a cool place until set. Refrigerate.*

2. *Trim the venison on an immaculately clean cutting board, removing any fat and veins. Finely dice the meat, cover well with plastic wrap and refrigerate. It is best to chop the meat as close to serving time as possible.*

3. *Peel the cooked beets and cut into julienne.*

4. *Make a vinaigrette with the canola oil, salt, mustard, maple syrup and the remaining cider vinegar.*

Assembly

5. *Twenty minutes before serving, combine the raw venison with the green onion and half the vinaigrette. Mix the beet julienne with a little vinaigrette and set aside. Cut the jelly into small cubes. Shave the cheese.*

6. *Arrange the beet julienne on chilled plates and top with the tartare. Surround with the greens and cheese shavings and sprinkle with cubes of jelly.*

Venison Tartare

Duo of Pan-seared Quail Supreme

and Fresh Duck Foie Gras with a Julienne of Hubbard Squash and Caramelized Onions

Quick, easy and irresistible, this recipe combines the luxury of foie gras and quail with the everyday taste of onions and squash. Of course, the marvellous mead from the Desrochers farm in Ferme-Neuve adds just the right touch.

4 SERVINGS

INGREDIENTS

2	large onions, thinly sliced	2
45 mL	butter	3 tbsp
45 mL	virgin olive oil	3 tbsp
	salt, to taste	
200 mL	Cuvée du Diable mead (**or** sweet, floral, oak-aged white wine)	¾ cup
300 mL	flavourful poultry stock (see page 18)	1 ¼ cups
250 mL	julienned Hubbard squash	1 cup
4	quail supremes (if quails purchased whole, save the legs for another recipe)	4
4	escalopes of fresh duck foie gras, 50 g (1 ¾ oz) each	4
	freshly ground pepper	

Preparation

1. In a skillet, caramelize the onions with a little butter and olive oil. Season with salt, remove from the skillet and keep warm.

2. Deglaze the skillet with the mead and poultry stock. Simmer to reduce by ⅔ or to a sauce consistency. Season to taste and set the finished sauce aside.

3. In another skillet, cook the julienned squash in a little butter over low heat for no more than 2 minutes. Keep warm.

Assembly

4. In a heavy skillet, heat a little butter and olive oil, then pan-sear the quail supremes over medium heat for 1 minute per side. Season with salt and keep warm.

5. Pan-sear the escalopes of foie gras the same way, also for 1 minute per side. Remove from the skillet and place on a rack. Season with salt and keep warm.

6. To serve, mix together the caramelized onions and julienned squash, and arrange a portion on each plate. Add a quail supreme, topped with an escalope of foie gras, to each serving. Sprinkle with freshly ground pepper and top with sauce. Serve immediately.

Duo of Pan-seared Quail Supreme

Monkfish Medallions
with Two-Mustard Veal Sauce, Cippolini Onions and Squash

 Monkfish may be ugly to look at but it has quite a firm, white, delicate-tasting flesh and few bones.

It may seem surprising to combine fish with a meat stock and mustard, but the flavours and textures complement each other amazingly well.

4 SERVINGS

INGREDIENTS

30 mL	Meaux mustard (grainy mustard)	2 tbsp
30 mL	Dijon mustard	2 tbsp
100 mL	extra-virgin olive oil	⅜ cup
12	small cippolini onions	12
60 mL	white wine	¼ cup
200 mL	veal stock (see page 18)	¾ cup
	salt, to taste	
	fresh lemon juice	
50 g	butter	1 ¾ oz
½	pepper squash, julienned	½
800 g	cleaned fresh monkfish fillets, cut into medallions	1 ¾ lb
	purslane for garnish	

Preparation

1. Combine the Meaux mustard and Dijon mustard with 3o mL (2 tbsp) olive oil. Set aside.

2. Peel and trim the onions. Set aside.

3. In a small saucepan, bring the white wine to a boil, and boil for 2 minutes. Add the veal stock and simmer to reduce by ⅔. Add 5 mL (1 tsp) of the mustard mixture and season with salt to taste. Add a few drops of lemon juice and and 15 mL (1 tbsp) butter. Keep warm over low heat.

Assembly

4. Sauté the onions in a skillet with 15 mL (1 tbsp) olive oil and 15 mL (1 tbsp) butter, over low heat, until soft and caramelized. Season with salt and keep warm.

5. Brown the julienned squash in 15 mL (1 tbsp) olive oil over high heat. Season with salt and set aside.

6. Heat the rest of the olive oil in a skillet. Over high heat, pan-sear the monkfish medallions until browned, about 2 minutes per side. Turn the heat to low for another minute or two until done, or until it is just about to come apart when probed. Season with salt. Brush with the mustard mixture.

7. To serve, divide the onions, the julienned squash and the monkfish medallions between four heated plates. Top with the sauce and garnish with purslane.

Monkfish Medallions

Pan-roasted Goose Supreme

with a Braised Leg and Foie Gras–stuffed Cabbage Roll, and Sautéed Cabbage with Orange Zest and Cranberries

❧ *Cabbage, flavourful farm-fresh goose and foie gras, citrus fruit and berries: a winning combination for a tasty and hearty winter recipe.*

6 SERVINGS

INGREDIENTS

1	goose from Baie du Febvre	1
1	large head of Savoy cabbage	1
½	red cabbage	½
100 mL	Cuvée du Diable mead (or sweet, floral, oak-aged white wine)	⅜ cup
	juice and zest of 1 orange	
2	shallots, chopped	2
6	fresh thyme sprigs	6
4	juniper berries	4
60 mL	cranberries (preferably wild)	¼ cup
	salt, to taste	
60 g	unsalted butter	2 oz
200 g	white mushrooms, thinly sliced	7 oz
200 g	fresh foie gras (duck or goose), cut into large cubes	7 oz
	extra-virgin olive oil	

Preparation

1. Remove the supremes from the goose. Trim the supremes and score the fat in a criss-cross pattern with a knife. Refrigerate.

2. Remove 6 large leaves from the Savoy cabbage to make the cabbage rolls. Blanch for a minute or two until malleable and brightly coloured, refresh in ice water, pat dry and set aside. Finely slice the rest of the Savoy cabbage and the red cabbage and set aside.

3. In a non-reactive roasting pan or casserole, braise the goose legs in the oven at 150 °C (300 °F) for 2 ½ hours, with the mead, orange juice, and half each of the zest, chopped shallots, thyme, juniper berries, cranberries and salt (the cabbage trimmings can also be added if desired, as can any goose bones, excluding excess skin or fat).

4. When done, remove the legs and debone them. Set the meat aside. Strain the cooking juices into a saucepan and skim the fat from the cooking juices. Add the remaining thyme, juniper berries and cranberries and cook over medium heat. Simmer to reduce slightly, and correct the seasoning. When done, whisk in 30 mL (2 tbsp) of the butter and keep warm.

5. To prepare the cabbage roll filling, sauté the sliced mushrooms and the remaining chopped shallots in 15 mL (1 tbsp) of butter over high heat. Season with salt and add a little zest. Place in a bowl and let cool. Add 300 mL (1 ¼ cups) deboned leg meat and the foie gras cubes. Mix and correct the seasoning.

6. Preheat the oven to 175 °C (350 °F). Spread out the cabbage leaves and place a little filling on each one. Roll the cabbage leaves to form tight little bundles. Place in a buttered ovenproof dish and bake for 20 minutes. Keep warm.

Assembly

7. In a heavy skillet, pan-fry the goose supremes, skin-side down, in a little olive oil over medium-high heat until nicely browned and crisp. Season with salt and keep warm over low heat. Sauté the sliced cabbage in a little olive oil and butter. Season with salt and add the remaining zest.

8. To serve, arrange the sliced cabbage, slices of goose supreme and cabbage rolls on heated plates. Top with the sauce.

Pan-roasted Goose Supreme

Old-fashioned Roasted Stuffed Quail

with Foie Gras, Mead Sauce and Six Spices

This is one of my oldest and most reliable recipes. It takes a little effort in the beginning, but it's easy to serve, and always pleases.

INGREDIENTS

STUFFING

4 slices	stale sourdough bread, coarsely crumbled	4 slices
250 mL	35% cream	1 cup
100 mL	Cuvée du Diable mead (or sweet, floral, oak-aged white wine)	⅜ cup
1	egg	1
1	shallot, minced	1
5 mL	ground spices, mixed (1 pinch each of black pepper, allspice, pink pepper, cardamom, star anise and juniper berries)	1 tsp
250 g	fresh duck foie gras, cubed	9 oz
	salt, to taste	

QUAILS

6	whole quails (wingtips, breastbone and back removed)	6
	salt, to taste	
75 g	unsalted butter, softened	2 ⅔ oz

SAUCE

150 mL	spiced mead caramel (see page 21)	⅝ cup
500 mL	quail or poultry stock (see page 18)	2 cups
	salt, to taste	
50 g	unsalted butter	1 ¾ oz

SPINACH

1 kg	fresh spinach	2 lb
15 mL	butter	1 tbsp
15 mL	extra-virgin olive oil	1 tbsp

Preparation

1. Preheat the oven to 190 °C (375 °F).

2. Place the bread in a bowl and add the cream and mead. Let stand for a few minutes. Add the egg, shallot, spices, foie gras and salt. Stir the stuffing mixture well. Correct the seasoning, if necessary.

3. Place the deboned quails, skin-side down, on a clean work surface. Season with salt and distribute the stuffing equally among them. Close, folding legs underneath, and place on squares of aluminum foil, leaving a 5 cm (2 in.) border around. Gather up the sides of the foil and tie with kitchen twine, leaving the breast exposed. Place in a shallow baking dish, breast-side up, and smear with the softened butter. Set aside.

4. Set aside 15 mL (1 tbsp) of the spiced mead caramel, then bring the rest to a boil in a medium-sized saucepan. Add the quail or poultry stock and simmer to reduce by ⅔. Season with salt to taste and set aside.

5. Place the quails in the oven and roast for about 20 minutes, or until the flesh is nicely browned and the juices are running clear. During the last 5 minutes, baste with the cooking juices and the reserved 15 mL (1 tbsp) spiced mead caramel. Let rest for 10 minutes in a warm place.

Assembly

6. In a saucepan, cook the spinach in a little butter and olive oil. Season with salt and set aside.

7. Return the saucepan containing the sauce to the stove to reheat, and season the sauce to taste. Remove from heat and finish the sauce by whisking in the butter.

8. Arrange the spinach on heated plates and place the quails on top. Top with the sauce.

Old-fashioned Roasted Stuffed Quail

Pork Tenderloin Medallions

with Paillot de Chèvre Cheese from Portneuf, Thyme-flavoured Root Vegetables and Aged Balsamic Shallot Sauce

 Paillot de Chèvre is a ripened goat's milk cheese moulded into a cylindrical shape. It is made by Fromagerie Cayer in St.-Raymond, Quebec. According to the Répertoire des fromages du Québec, this Paillot de Chèvre is made only with goat's milk, and its pleasantly sharp taste goes particularly well with pork.

4 SERVINGS

Ingredients

1	small celery root, peeled	1
1	medium carrot, peeled	1
1	large parsnip, peeled	1
	fresh thyme sprigs	
	salt, to taste	
2	pork tenderloins, sliced into twelve 2.5-cm (1-in.) medallions	2
30 mL	butter	2 tbsp
15 mL	extra-virgin olive oil	1 tbsp
125 g	butter, cut into pieces	4 ½ oz
4	shallots, minced	4
75 mL	balsamic vinegar (aged minimum 10 years)	5 tbsp
200 mL	red wine	¾ cup
125 mL	veal stock (see page 18)	½ cup
120 g	Paillot de Chèvre (or other ripened goat cheese), cut into 12 discs	4 ¼ oz

Preparation

1. *Finely dice the root vegetables. Place them in a saucepan, cover with salted water and boil until tender. Drain. Add the thyme and season with salt to taste. Keep warm.*

2. *In a skillet, pan-sear the pork medallions in 30 ml (1 tbsp) butter and the olive oil, 2 minutes per side, over medium heat. Remove the medallions from the skillet and keep warm.*

3. *Add a little butter to the same skillet and sauté the shallots until golden brown. Deglaze with the balsamic vinegar and red wine. Add the veal stock and simmer*

to reduce by half. Season with salt to taste, add a bit more butter and set aside.

Assembly

4. *Place the pork medallions on a baking sheet and top with the cheese slices. Broil in the oven until the cheese starts to melt.*

5. *Arrange root vegetables in the centre of the heated plates, placing three pork medallions per plate around them, and top with the sauce.*

Pork Tenderloin
Medallions

ANNE DESJARDINS COOKS AT L'EAU À LA BOUCHE
THE SEASONAL CUISINE OF QUEBEC

Victor et Berthold *Cheese*

Melted on Sourdough Bread with Cumin Carrot Chutney and Mirabel Greens

The sweet and sour chutney will keep in the refrigerator for several weeks. I make it with multi-coloured carrots grown by Terry Hussey of Insalada, but any variety you like will work fine. It is a tasty accompaniment for a strong flavoured, semi-firm, washed-rind cheese like Victor et Berthold, or with charcuterie and rillettes (sliced deli meats and pâtés) as an appetizer.

4 SERVINGS

INGREDIENTS

5 mL	cumin seeds	1 tsp
125 mL	honey	½ cup
125 mL	natural cider vinegar	½ cup
1 pinch	turmeric	1 pinch
1	onion, finely diced	1
6	large carrots, grated or finely julienned	6
200 g	Victor et Berthold cheese	7 oz
4	slices sourdough bread, toasted	4
50 g	salad greens	1 ¾ oz sel

PREPARATION

1. In a medium-sized pan, toast the cumin seeds for 1 minute over low heat.

2. Add the honey, cider vinegar and turmeric and mix well. Then add the onions and carrots, and cook until the onions are translucent and the carrots tender but still firm.

3. Refrigerate the chutney.

ASSEMBLY

4. Place 50 g (1 ¾ oz) cheese on each slice of toast. Place under the broiler to melt the cheese.

5. Serve with salad greens and the cumin carrot chutney.

Honey Delights

I have many different recipes featuring honey, largely inspired by the wonderful products from the Desrochers farm in Ferme-Neuve. This dish features three recipes together in one elaborate dessert that highlights honey's many different forms and textures, both hot and cold. This is a crowd pleaser at the restaurant. Feel free to try only one recipe and serve larger portions, or serve all three but lighten the workload by purchasing a good honey ice cream for the frappé. Both the frozen nougatine and the crème brûlée can be made in advance. Just be sure to use a good-quality, aromatic honey.

Frozen Nougatine

6 SERVINGS

INGREDIENTS

	NOUGATINE	
85 g	icing sugar	⅓ cup
15 mL	water	1 tbsp
50 g	slivered almonds	2 oz
160 mL	35% cream	½ cup
85 g	granulated sugar	⅓ cup
15 mL	water	1 tbsp
70 g	egg whites (2 to 3 large)	2 ½ oz
	HONEY MOUSSE	
100 g (75 mL)	honey	⅓ cup
1 leaf (2 g)	gelatin, soaked in cold water, squeezed dry	1 leaf (¼ pkg)
3	egg yolks	3
170 mL	35% cream	⅔ cup

Preparation

1. Make a caramel with the first 2 ingredients.

2. Stir in the slivered almonds and spread the mixture quickly and evenly on parchment paper. Allow to set into a nougatine. Once cool, it is ready.

3. Whip the 160 mL (½ cup) cream to soft peaks.

4. Combine 85 g (⅓ cup) granulated sugar with 15 mL (1 tbsp) water and heat to 121°C (250°F).

5. Whip the egg whites to soft peaks, then slowly stir in the hot syrup from step 4 to make an Italian meringue. Whip until the meringue has cooled down.

6. Put the nougatine from step 2 in a food processor; pulse until fine and fold into the meringue.

7. Fold the whipped cream into the nougatine and mix in gently until well blended.

8. Line small round moulds (4 cm [1 ½ in.] in diameter) with wax paper to prevent nougatine from sticking when frozen. Fill moulds to a little more than half full with the mixture. Freeze until solid.

9. For the honey mousse, bring the honey to a boil and add the softened gelatin. Remove from heat.

10. Beat the egg yolks with a mixer, pouring in the warm honey until the mixture has cooled down.

11. Whip the 170 mL (⅔ cup) cream to soft peaks, and fold into the honey-egg mixture.

12. Pour into the moulds over the frozen nougatine and place in the freezer.

Note

This recipe should be prepare a day ahead.

Honey Delights

Honey Crème Brûlée

8 SMALL (75 mL [2 OZ]) RAMEKINS

INGREDIENTS

90 mL	wildflower honey	⅓ cup
200 mL	whole milk	¾ cup
300 mL	35% cream	1 ¼ cups
6	egg yolks, beaten	6
60 mL	sugar	4 tbsp

PREPARATION

1. Bring the honey, milk and cream to a boil in a small saucepan. Pour in the beaten egg yolks, while whisking gently.

2. Cook the mixture over low heat, stirring constantly, to 85°C (180°F) or until the egg proteins have coagulated and the mixture is thick. Remove from heat, and set the pan into an ice bath to stop the cooking. Pour the mixture into ramekins and allow to cool. (If you do not have an instant-read thermometer, and if time allows, bake the crème brûlées in the oven instead of on the stovetop. To do this, pour the mixture into ramekins and cook in a 120°C (250°F) oven for 40 minutes or until custard is set. Remove from oven, allow to cool.) Cover with plastic wrap and refrigerate.

Honey Frappé

6 LARGE (100 ML [3OZ]) SHOOTER GLASSES

INGREDIENTS

75 g	granulated sugar	2 ⅔ oz
3	egg yolks	3
500 mL	whole milk	2 cups
60 mL	wildflower honey	¼ cup
250 mL	L'envolée mead (or dry floral white wine)	1 cup
	edible flowers for garnish	

PREPARATION

1. Cream the sugar and egg yolks in a medium-size bowl.

2. Bring the milk and honey to a boil in a saucepan, then add to the egg mixture and mix well. Return the mixture to the saucepan and heat to 80 °C (176°F) until the cream thickens and coats the back of a spoon. Cool, and then freeze in an ice cream maker, according to manufacturer's instructions.

3. To serve, mix the mead and the honey ice cream in a blender and serve immediately in frosted glasses.

Assembly

4. Sprinkle each crème brûlée (one at a time) with 5 mL (1 tsp) sugar, and caramelize with a blowtorch or heat for 30 seconds under the broiler. Remove the nougatine from the freezer and serve alongside. Add the frappé, and garnish the whole serving with some flowers from the garden. Serve on one large plate, or serve in succession, in the tasting menu style. Honey never tasted so good.

**ANNE DESJARDINS
COOKS AT
L'EAU À LA BOUCHE**
THE SEASONAL CUISINE
OF QUEBEC

PAGE 188

Index

Recipes by season
Spring

Index

Recipes by season
Spring

Summer

Fall

Winter

**ANNE DESJARDINS
COOKS AT
L'EAU À LA BOUCHE**
THE SEASONAL CUISINE
OF QUEBEC

PAGE 191

ACKNOWLEDGEMENTS

First, thanks to my father, Claude Desjardins, and my mother, Françoise, without whom this great adventure would never have taken place. Their support allowed the birth and development of a small rural eatery.

Thank you to Pierre Audette, my friend, my spouse and my partner, who has now shared with me more than twenty years of highs and lows in the hospitality business. Thanks also to my two sons: Félix, who has the patience of an angel and, especially, Emmanuel, who now works with us in the kitchen and who patiently and ably assisted with the food styling for the photos in this book.

Thanks to the restaurant and hotel staff at L'eau à la Bouche, especially Richard Poirier, Guy Lelièvre and Pierre Beaudin, who, as always, participate in this frenetic lifestyle with professionalism and who encourage both my folly and my passion.

I'd like also to mention the collaborators, assistants, cooks who work or have worked with me over the years: each one, in his or her way has contributed to the evolution and success of L'eau à la Bouche. I can't begin to name all of them but I won't forget any of them. More than anyone, I'd like to thank my sous-chef, Nancy Hinton, for her talent and for the generosity with which she shares her knowledge.

I'd like to highlight the work of the food producers and artisans in this region—my big food-producing family—for the quality of their products and for their perseverance. Thanks to those who opened their doors during the photo shoot for this book and also to Jean Audette, commissioner of the Table de concertation agroalimentaire des Laurentides.

AND SPECIAL THANKS TO:

Claude and Marie-Claude Desrochers of the Ferme Apicole Desrochers in Ferme-Neuve

Francine Beauséjour of Le P'tit train du Nord cheese dairy in Mont-Laurier

Sylvie D'Amours of the Centre d'interprétation de la Courage du Québec farm in St.-Joseph-du-Lac

Jude Lavigne of Verger Jud'Pom in Oka

Daniel Baillard of Fines Herbes par Daniel greenhouses in Mirabel

Yannick Achim of the Fromagerie du Marché in St.-Jérôme

Terry Hussey, Insalada's market gardener, in Prévost

François Brouillard of Jardins Sauvages in St.-Roch-de-l'Achigan

Denis Ferrer of Fermes Harpur, the stag of Boileau